Pedro Waloschek (Hrsg.)

Iutta und die Physiker
 y los Físicos – and the Physicists
95 **Zeichnungen** – *dibujos* – Drawings

Umschlagbilder
Imágenes cubierta
Cover pictures

Front:

iutta: „Albert Einstein"

Back:

Foto (Porträt) „iutta": Andrés Ludewig (Buenos Aires)

Ballonflüge zur Untersuchung der Höhenstrahlung.
Kolorierte Tuschezeichnung (1985).

Vuelos de balones para la investigacion de la radiacion cósmica.
Dibujo en tinta china coloreado (1985).

Balloon flights to investigate cosmic rays.
Coloured china ink drawing (1985).

iutta

und die Physiker

y los Físicos

and the Physicists

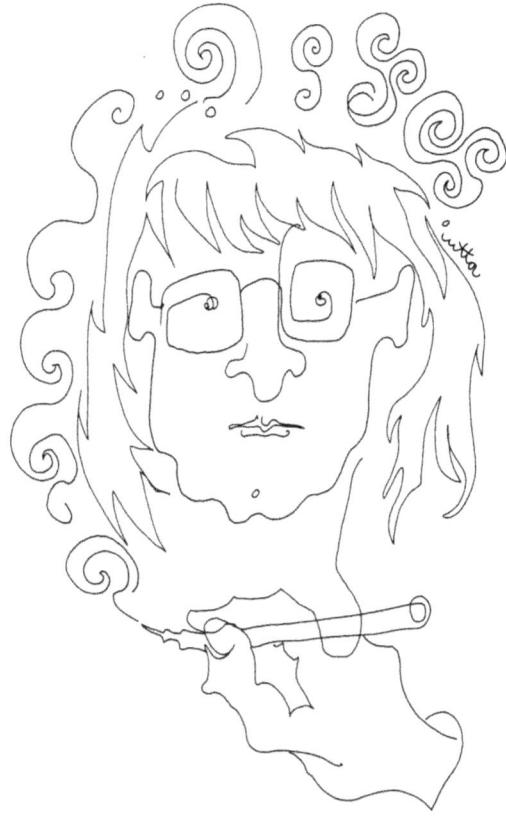

95

Zeichnungen
dibujos
Drawings

Zusammengestellt und herausgegeben von
Compilado y editado por – Compiled and edited by

Pedro Waloschek

Atelier OpaL Productions

Impressum

Die Deutsche Bibliothek – CIP-Einheitsaufnahme

Die Deutsche Bibliothek verzeichnet diese Publikation in der Deutschen Nationalbibliographie; detaillierte bibliographische Daten sind im Internet über <http://dnb.ddb.de> abrufbar.

Originalausgabe, 1. Auflage

All rights reserved

Copyright © 2005 Pedro Waloschek,
Achter Lüttmoor 45, D - 22559 Hamburg

Copyright (Zeichnungen - *Dibujos* - Drawings) © 2005 Jutta Waloschek,
Sonnenuhrgasse 1, 12a, A - 1060 Wien

Alle Rechte vorbehalten. Dieses Werk sowie alle seine Teile sind urheberrechtlich geschützt. Jede Verwertung in anderen als den gesetzlich zugelassenen Fällen ist ohne vorherige schriftliche Zustimmung der Inhaber der Rechte nicht zulässig.

Die englischen Texte wurden freundlicherweise von Karen Waloschek (Thorney, GB) überarbeitet, die spanischen von Ana Memelsdorff (Buenos Aires).

Satz, Layout, Umschlaggestaltung und Vorbereitung für den Druck:
Atelier OpaL Productions – Hamburg

Herstellung und Verlag: Books on Demand GmbH, Norderstedt

Gedruckt auf umweltfreundlichen, säure-, holz- und chlorfreiem sowie alterungsbeständigem Papier ISO 9706.

Im Buchhandel und Interntet-Shops zu bestellen (Ladenpreis: 8,- Euro).

ISBN 3-8334-2849-X

Inhalt – *Índice* – Contents

Einführung – *Introducción* – Introduction
7

Physiker bei der Arbeit
Físicos en acción
Physicists at Work
9

Die globalisierten Physiker
Los físicos globalizados
The Globalized Physicists
29

Physikerporträts
Retratos de Físicos
Physicists' Portraits
41

Verzeichnis – *Índice* – Index
101

iuttas in Kürze
iutta en breve
Short Curriculum Vitae
103

5

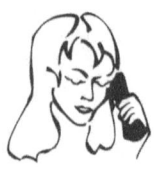 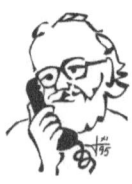

**Barbara & Pedro,
vor dem „Besuch im Teilchenzoo".**
preparando la visita al zoo de partículas.
preparing the visit to the particles zoo.

Einführung

Das Illustrieren von Büchern ist eine der vielen künstlerischen Tätigkeiten meiner Schwester Jutta (iutta). Die meisten ihrer hier vorgestellten Zeichnungen wurden in zwei meiner Bücher (*) veröffentlicht. Darin wird die Teilchenphysik und ihre Entwicklung im 20. Jahrhundert möglichst allgemein verständlich dargestellt. Die Illustrationen wurden im Rahmen intensiver Gespräche entwickelt, wobei vorhandene Fotos und Grafiken und einige Laborbesuche eine wichtige Rolle gespielt haben.

Introducción

La ilustración de libros es una de las muchas actividades artísticas de mi hermana Jutta (iutta). La mayor parte de los dibujos presentados aquí fueron publicados en dos de mis libros (*) (ambos en alemán). Se trata de introducciones populares a la física de partículas y de su evolución en el siglo 20. Las ilustraciones representan el resultado de intensos cambios de ideas, teniendo en cuenta fotos y dibujos ya existentes. Algunas visitas a laboratorios fueron de gran utilidad.

Introduction

Illustrating books is one of my sister Jutta's (iutta) many artistic activities. Most of the drawings shown here were previously published in two books I wrote for the general public (both in German) on particle physics and its development in the 20th century. Her illustrations are based on the many conversations we had concerning each of them before we were able to achieve the desired results. Photographs, drawings and Jutta's visits to laboratories were also helpful and inspiring.

Pedro Waloschek, April 2005

(*) „Der Multimensch" ECON-Verlag (1986),
„Besuch im Teilchenzoo" ro-ro-ro-sachbuch (1996).

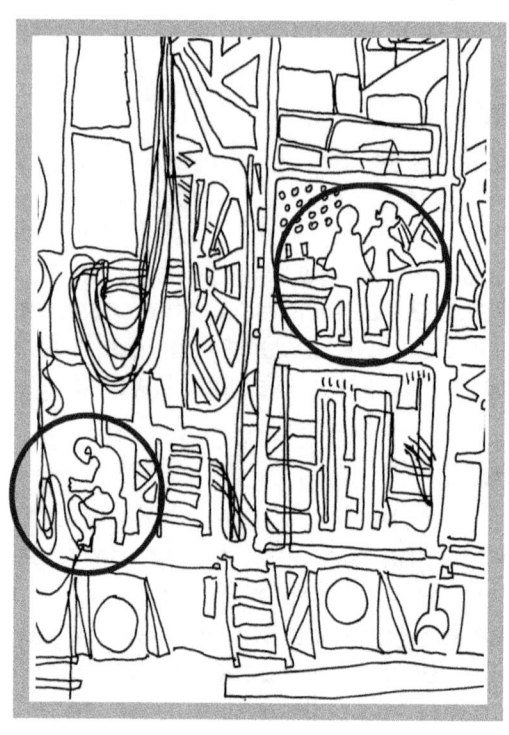

Physiker bei der Arbeit

Físicos en acción

Physicists at Work

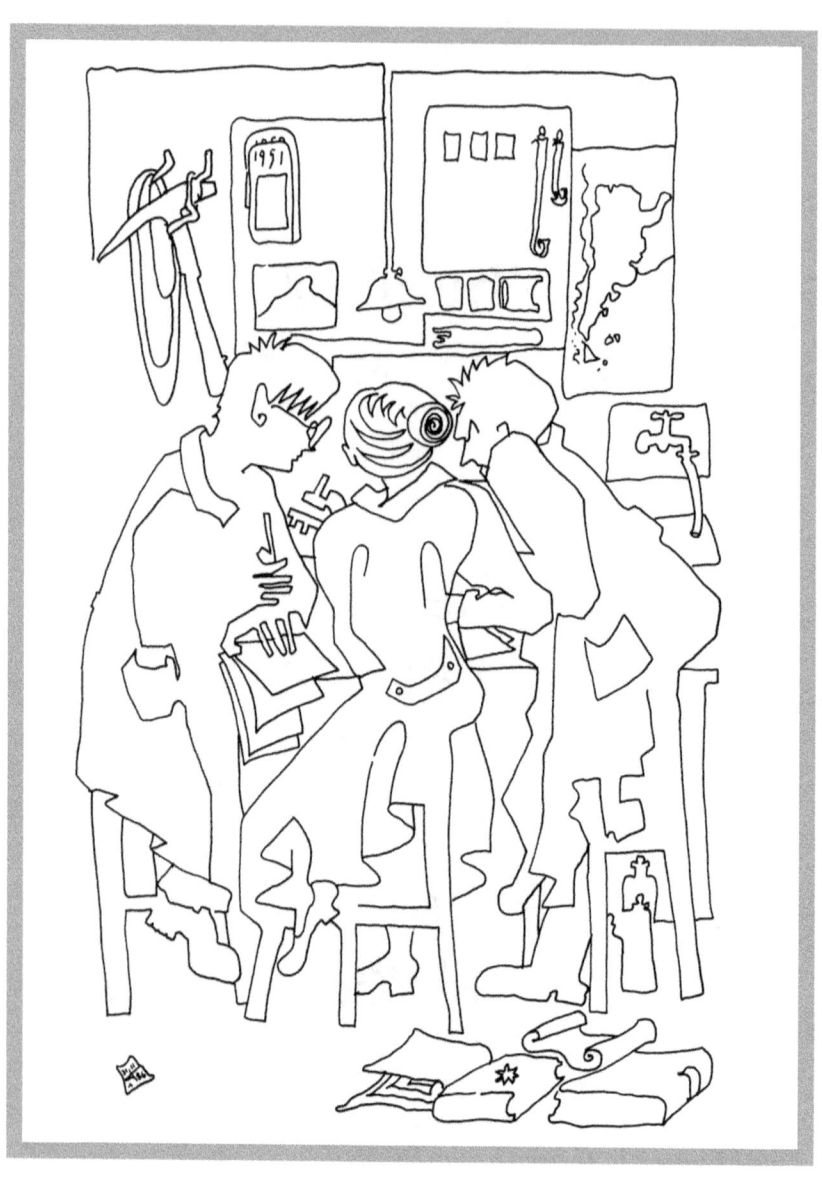

Vorbereitung einer Andenexpedition (Höhenstrahlung).
Preparación de una expedición a los Andes (radiación cósmica).
Preparing an expedition to the Andes (cosmic ray studies).
Buenos Aires 1951

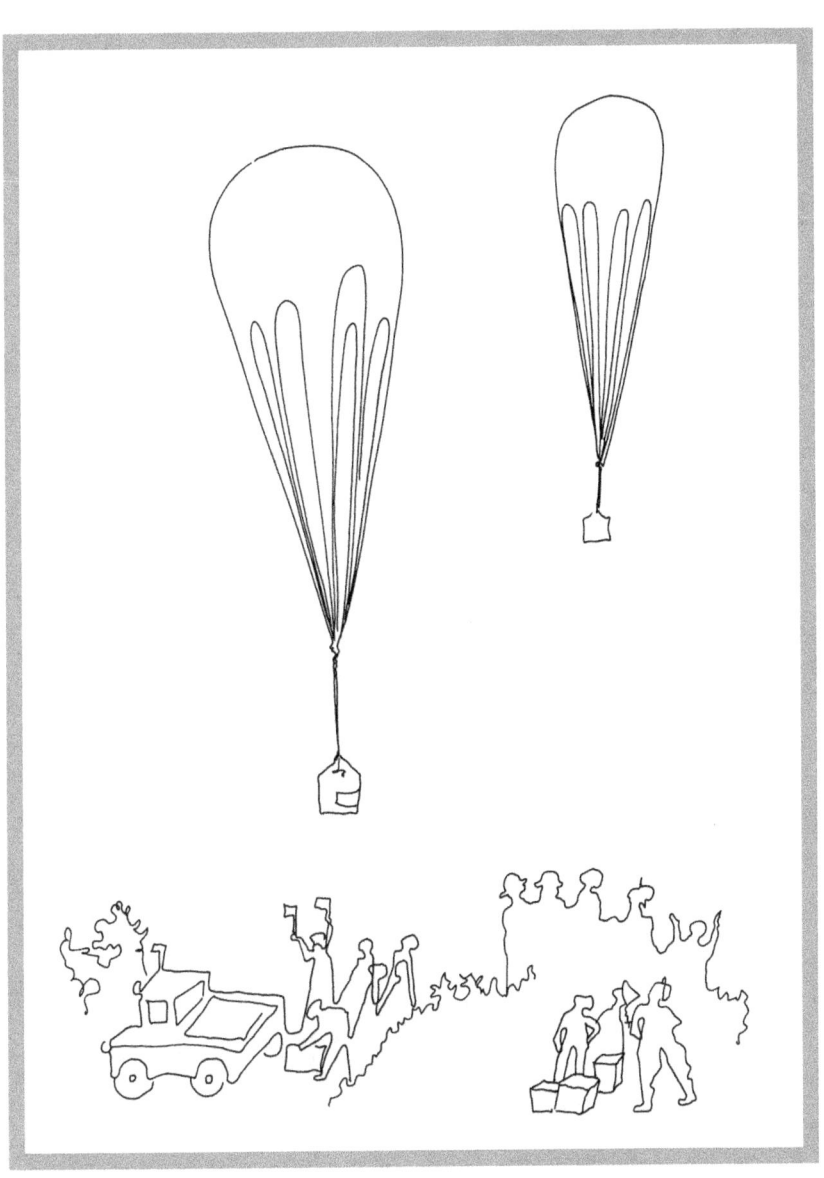

Ballonflüge zur Untersuchung der Höhenstrahlung.
Vuelos de balones para investigar la radiación cósmica.
Bolloon flights to investigate cosmic radiation.
Italia 1952

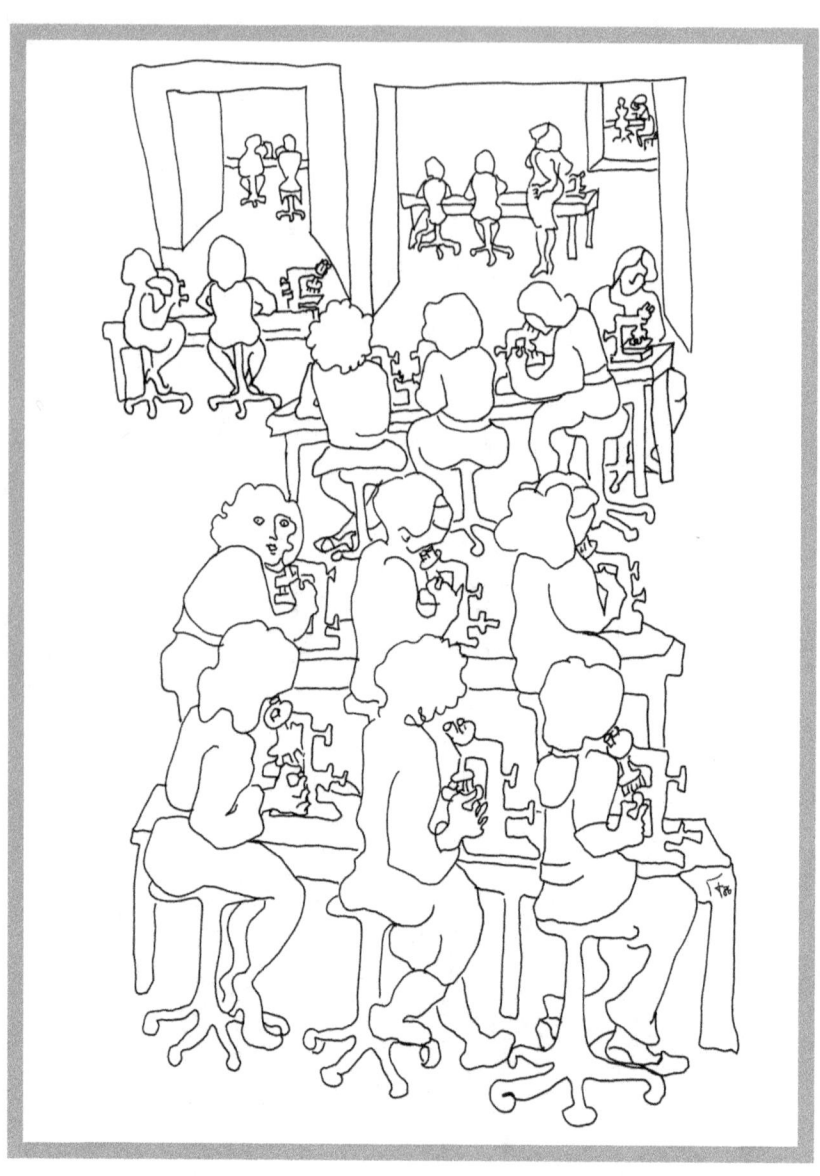

Scannen von Kernphotoplatten (Mikroskopierraum).
Análisis de placas nucleares (sala de microscopía).
Scanning nuclear emulsions (microscopes room).
Göttingen 1955

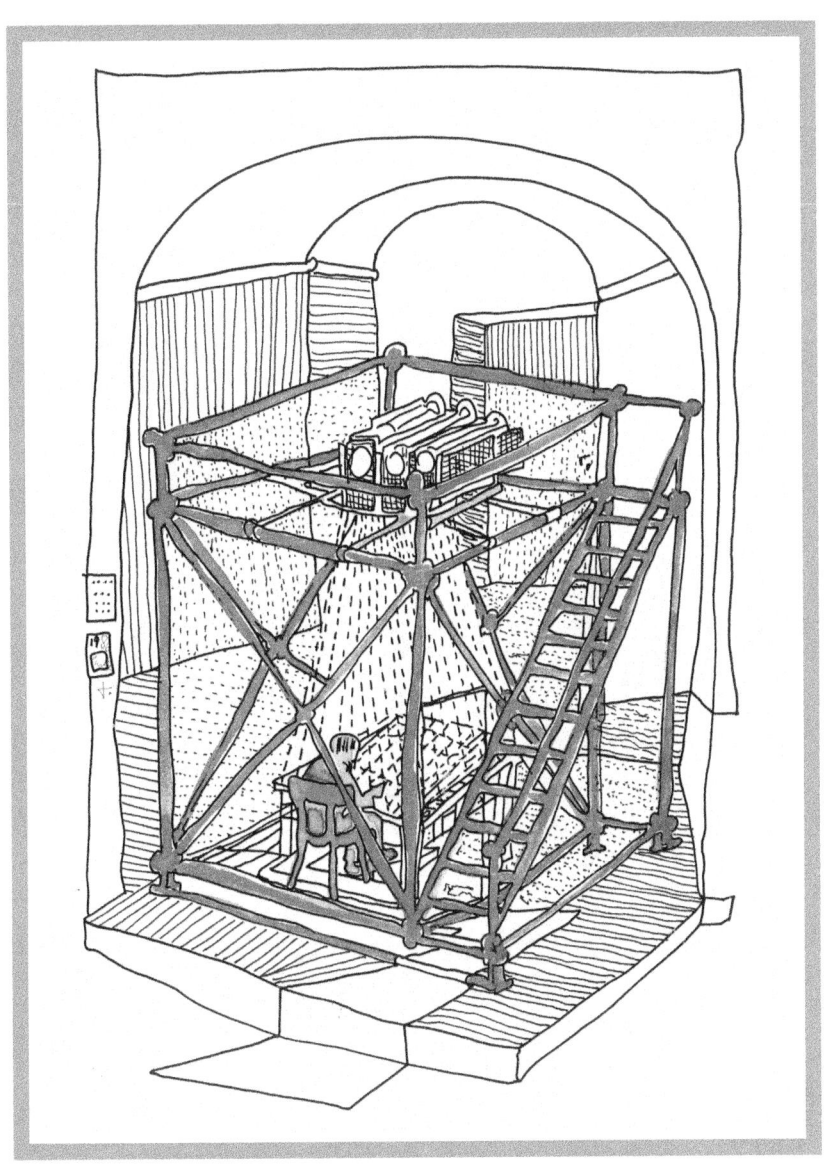

Analyse von Blasenkammerbilden.
Análisis de fotografías de cámara de burbujas.
Analysis of bubble chamber pictures.
Bologna 1957

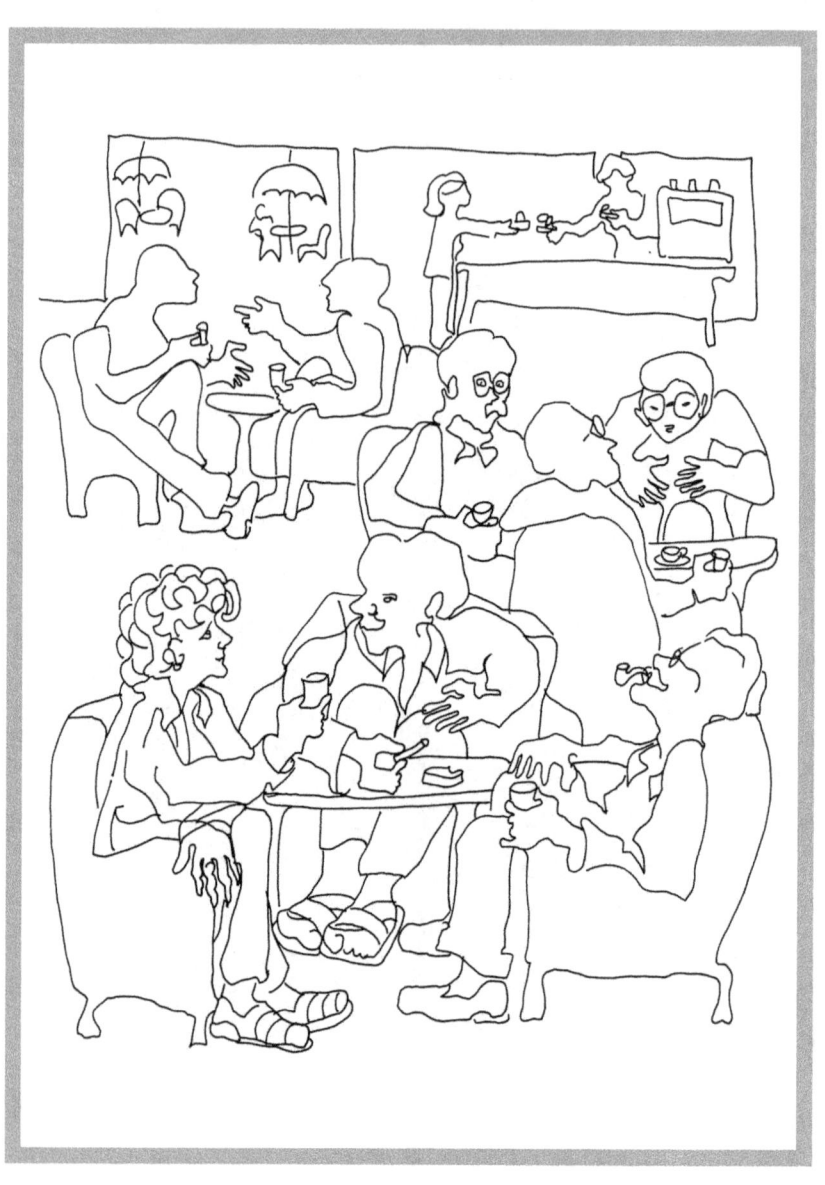

Kreative Entspannung in der Cafeteria des CERN.
Reposo creativo en la cafetería del CERN.
Creative relax in the CERN cafeteria.

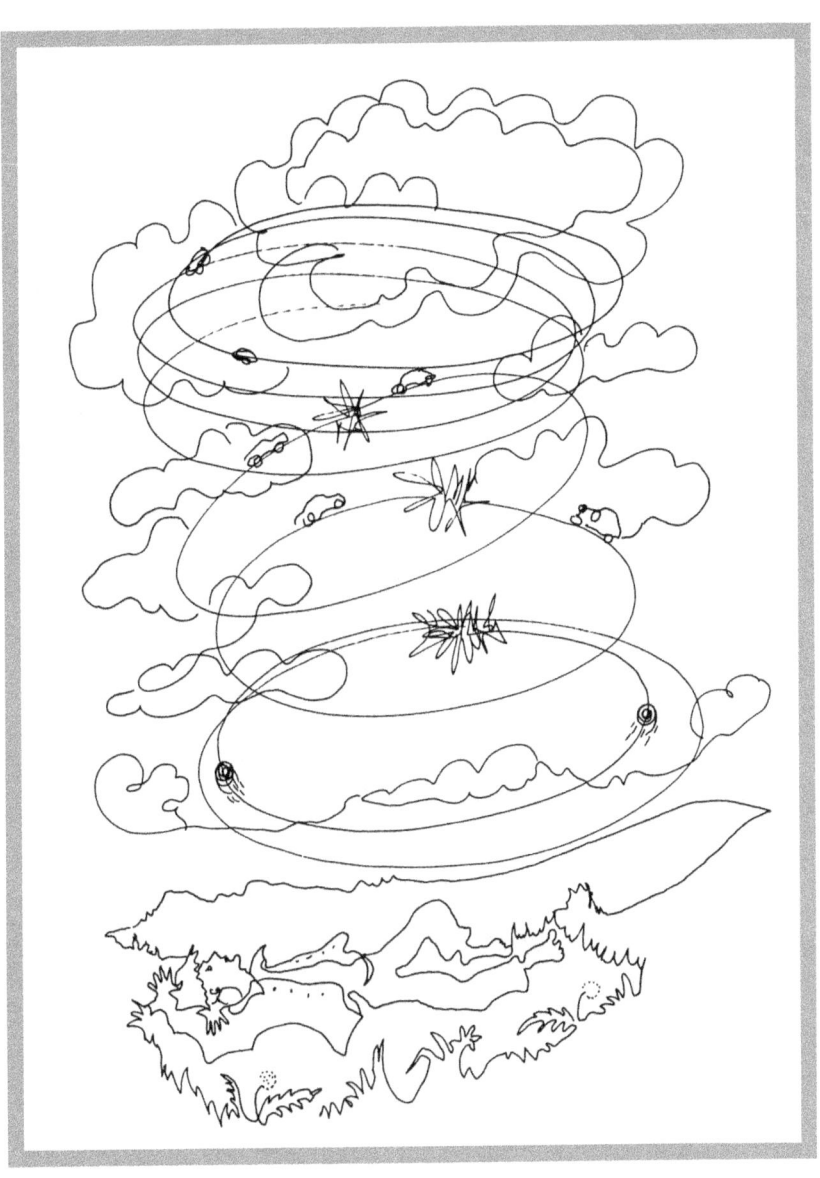

Rolf Wideröe erfindet den Speicherring-Collider.
Rolf Wideröe inventa los anillos de acumulación (collider).
Rolf Wideröe inventing the storage ring collider.
Norwegen 1943

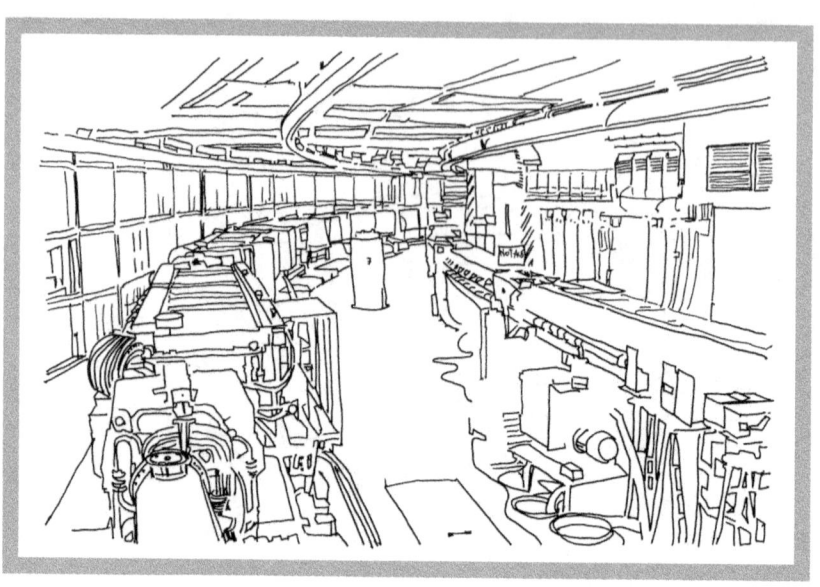

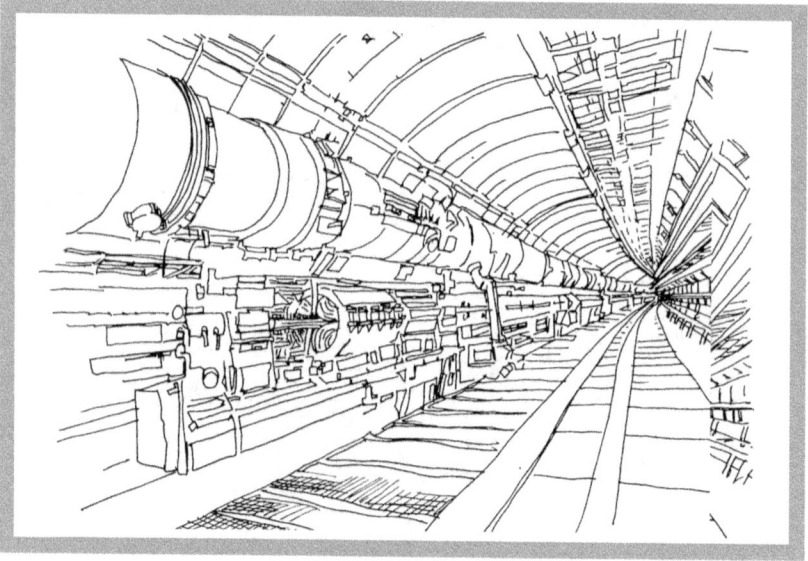

Oben: Zwei Synchrotrons. Unten: Der HERA-Tunnel.
Arriba: Dos sincrotrones. Abajo: El túnel de HERA.
Above: Two synchrotrons; below: The HERA tunnel.
DESY, Hamburg.

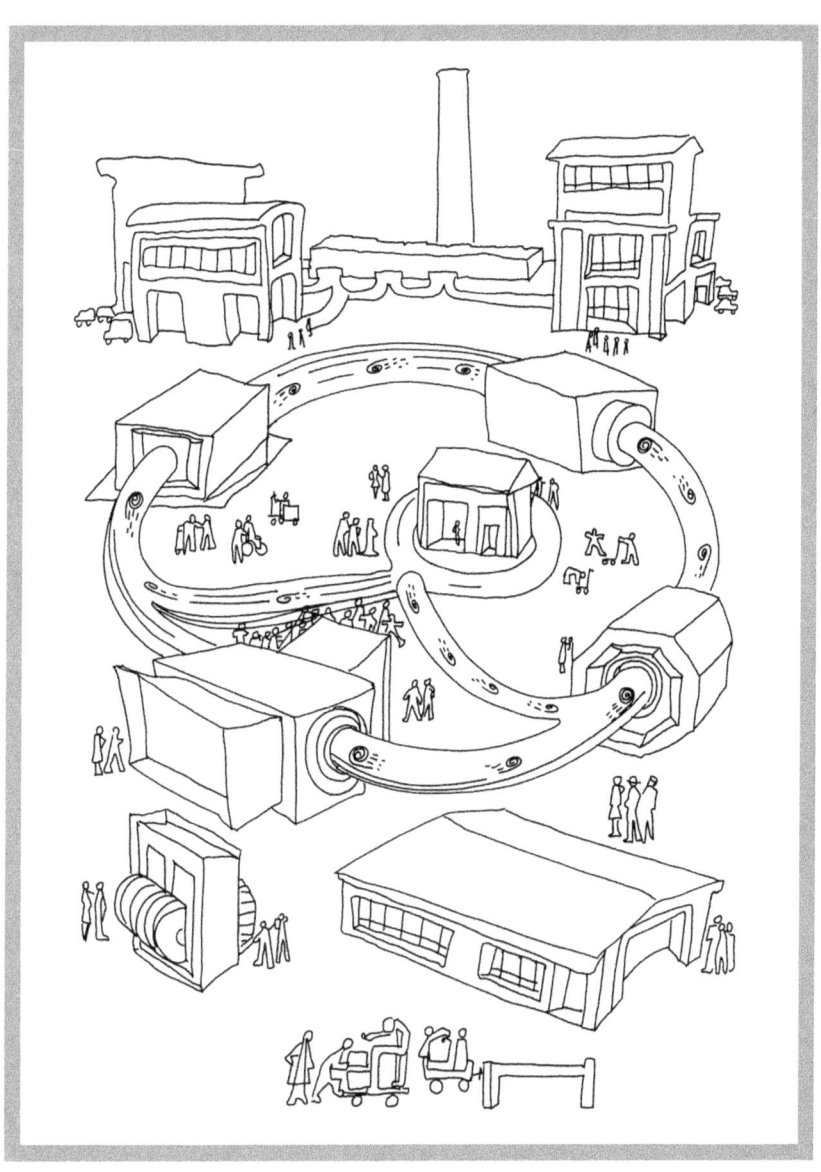

Beschleuniger-Labor mit Speicherring.
Laboratorio con aceleradores y anillo de acumulación.
Laboratory with accelerators and storage ring.

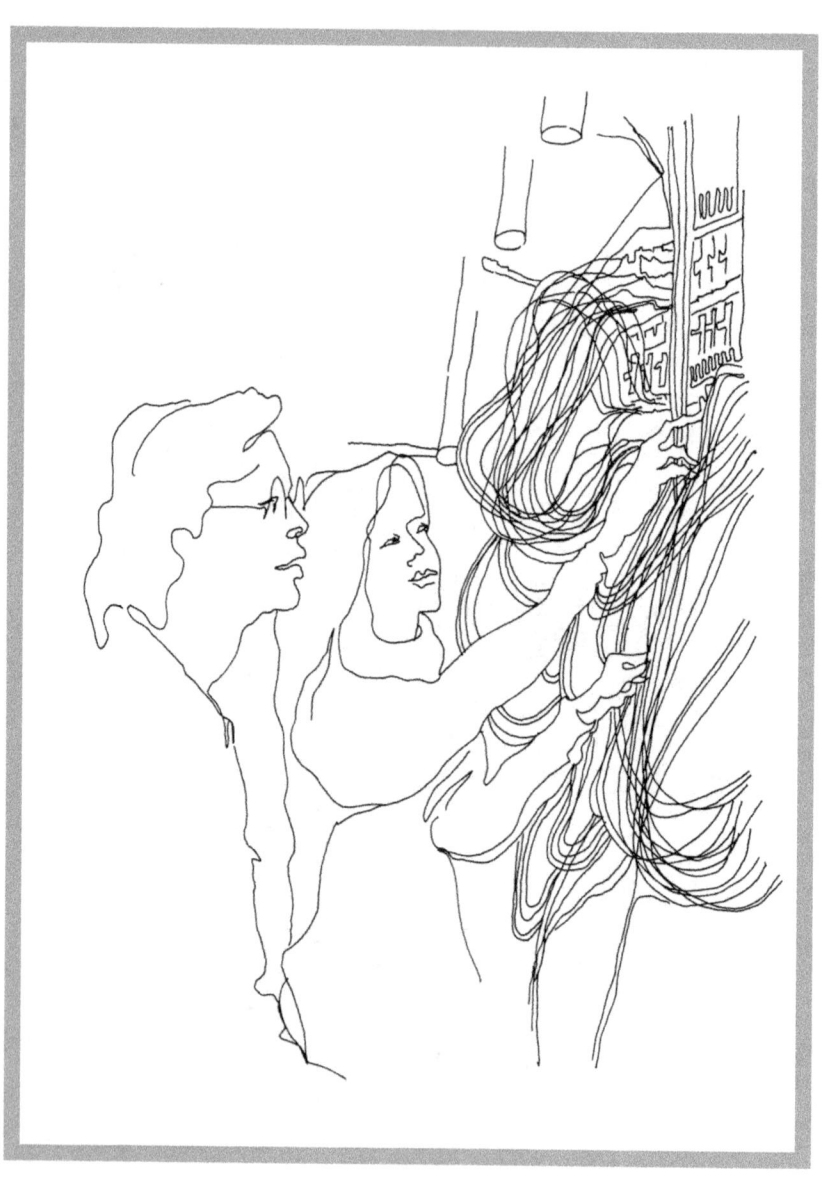

Verdrahtung der Elektronik eines Experiments.
Conectando cables en la electrónica de un experimento.
Cabling the electronics of an experiment.

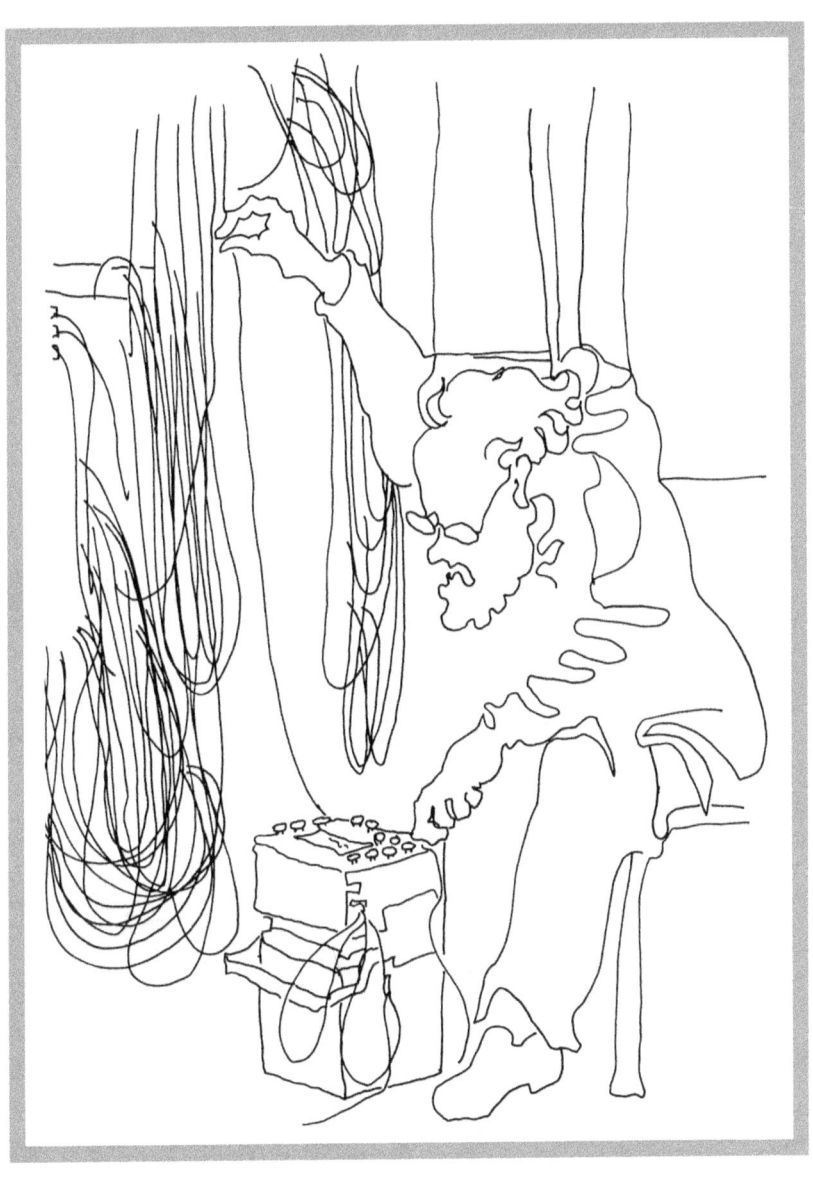

Zeit-Justierung der Komponenten des Experiments.
Ajustando el „timing" de componentes del experimento.
Adjusting the timing of the components of an experiment.

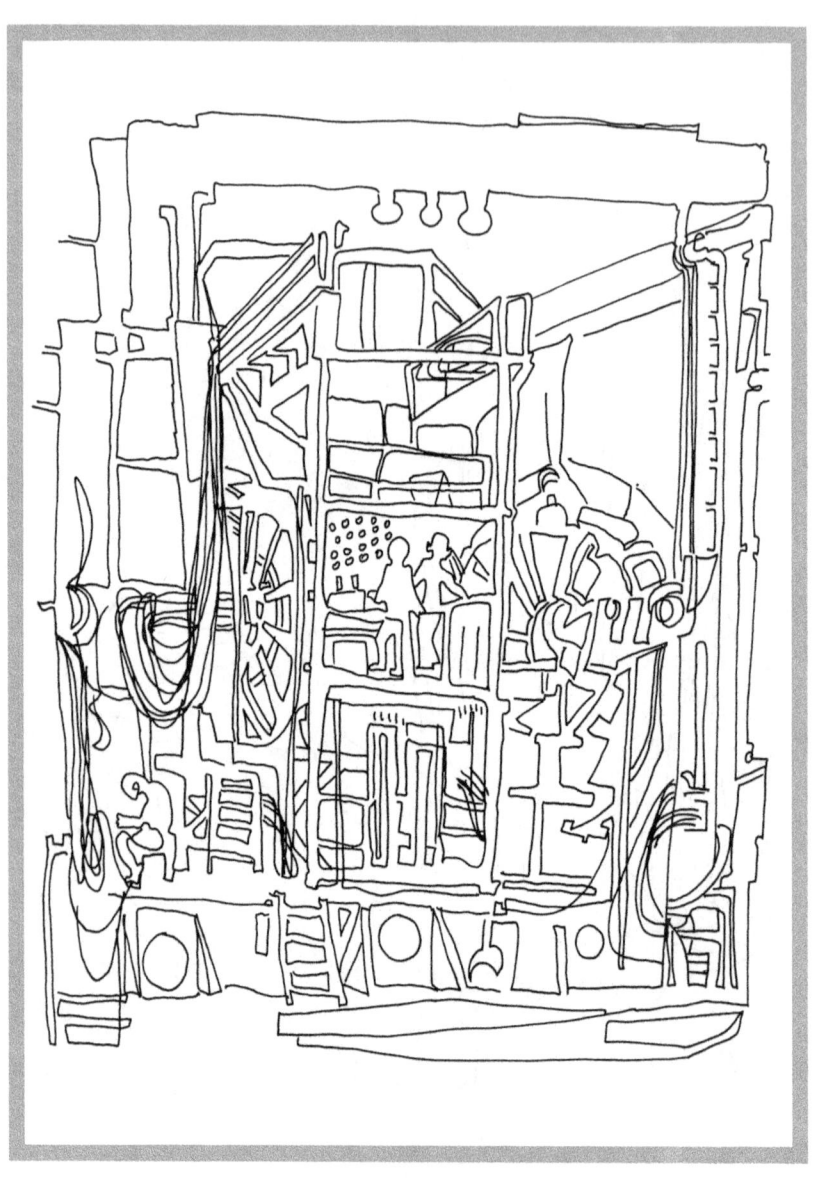

Aufbau eines Großexperiments am Speicherring.
Montaje de un experimento en un anillo de acumulación.
Setting up a storage ring experiment..
H1 at HERA, DESY, Hamburg

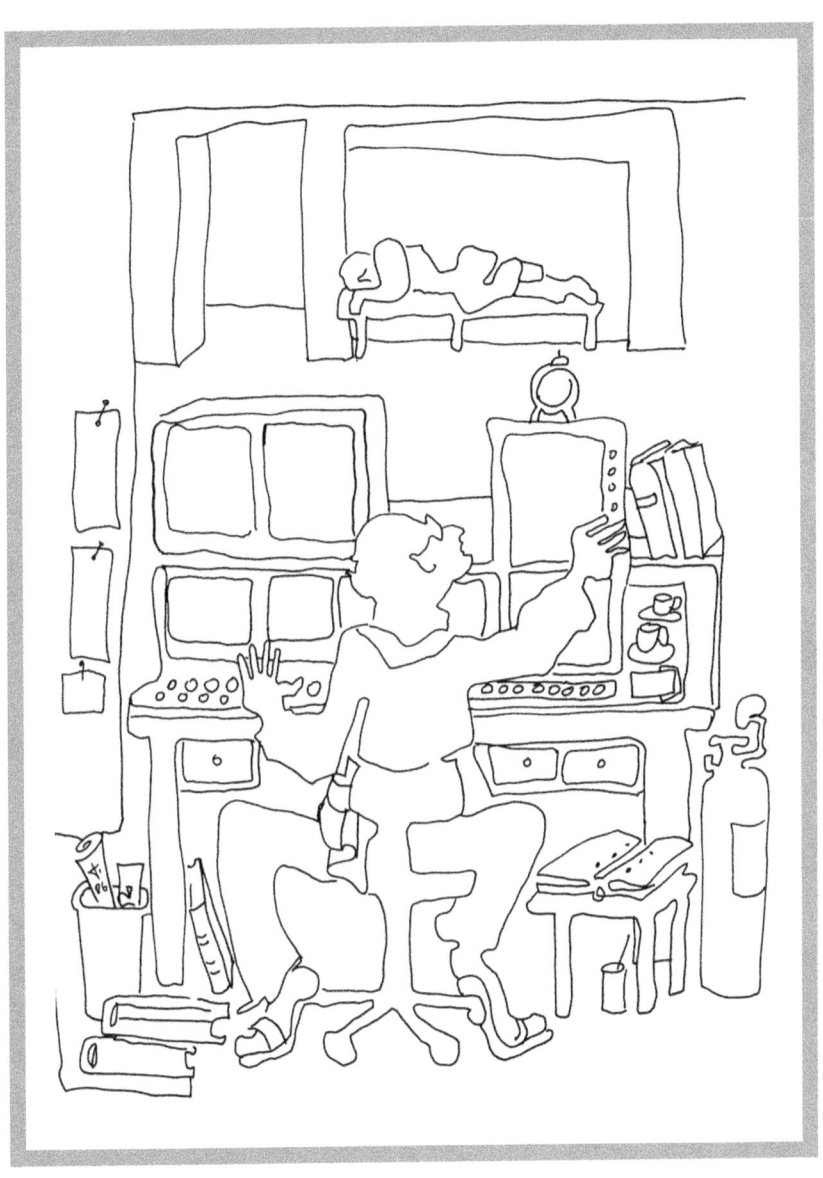

Schichtbetrieb an einem laufenden Experiment.
Físicos „de turno" en un experimento en función.
Physicist „on shift" at a running experiment.

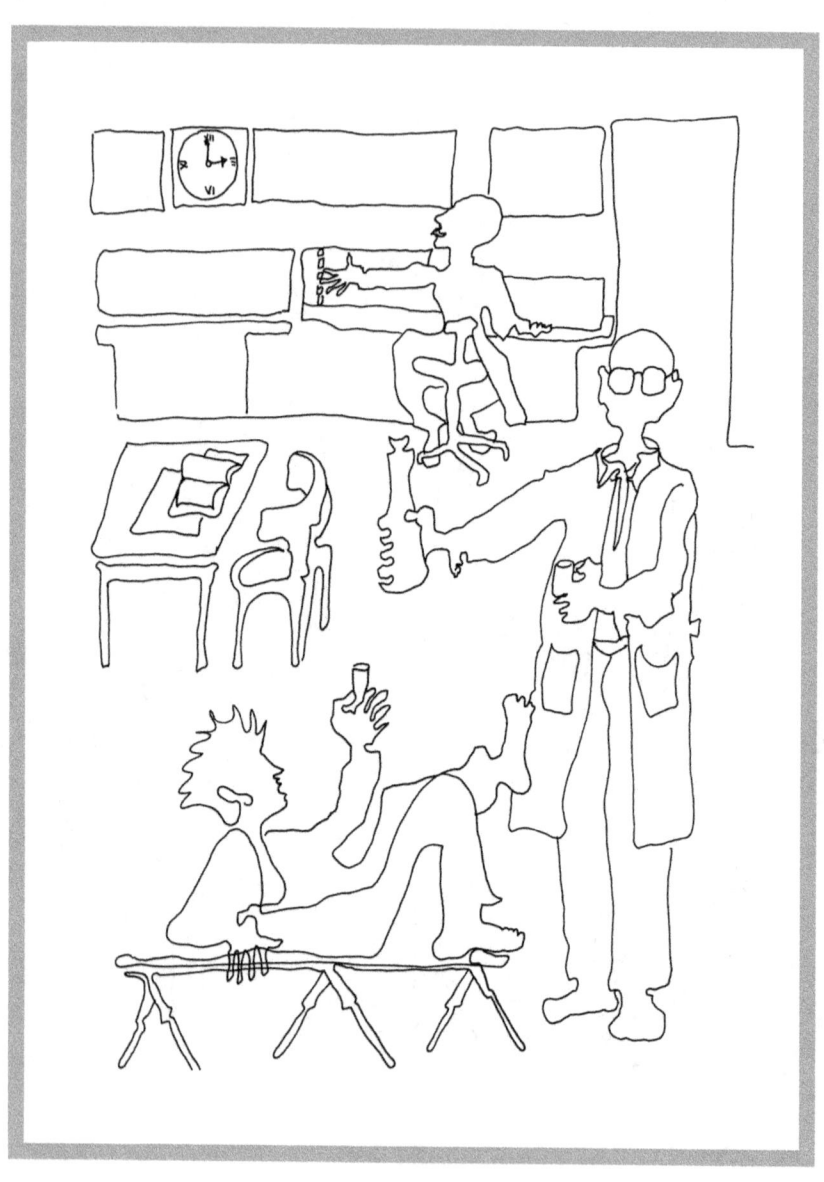

Erfolgreiches Schichtende. Kontrollraum, um 3 Uhr früh.
Exitoso fin de turno. Sala de control, a las 3 de la mañana.
The shift was successful; controll room, 3am.

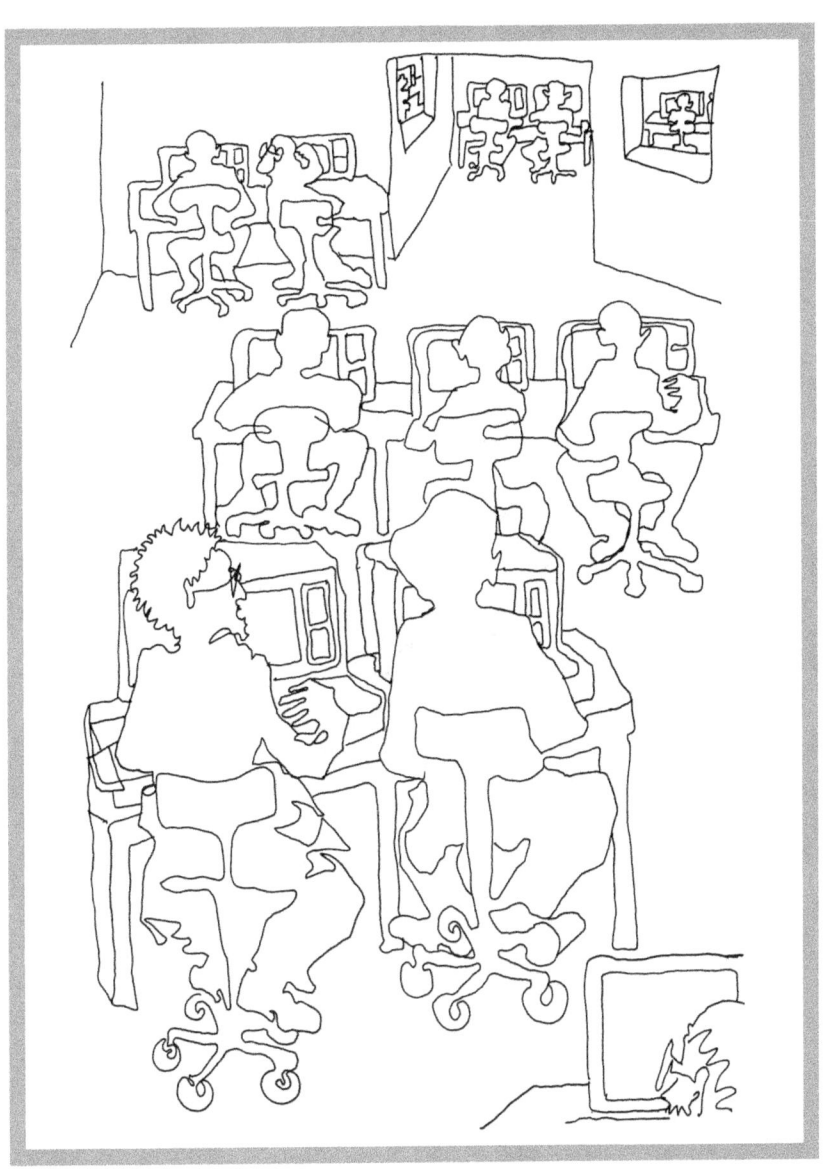

Physiker im Terminalraum des Rechenzentrums.
Físicos en la sala de terminales del centro de cálculo.
Physicists in the terminals room of the computing center.

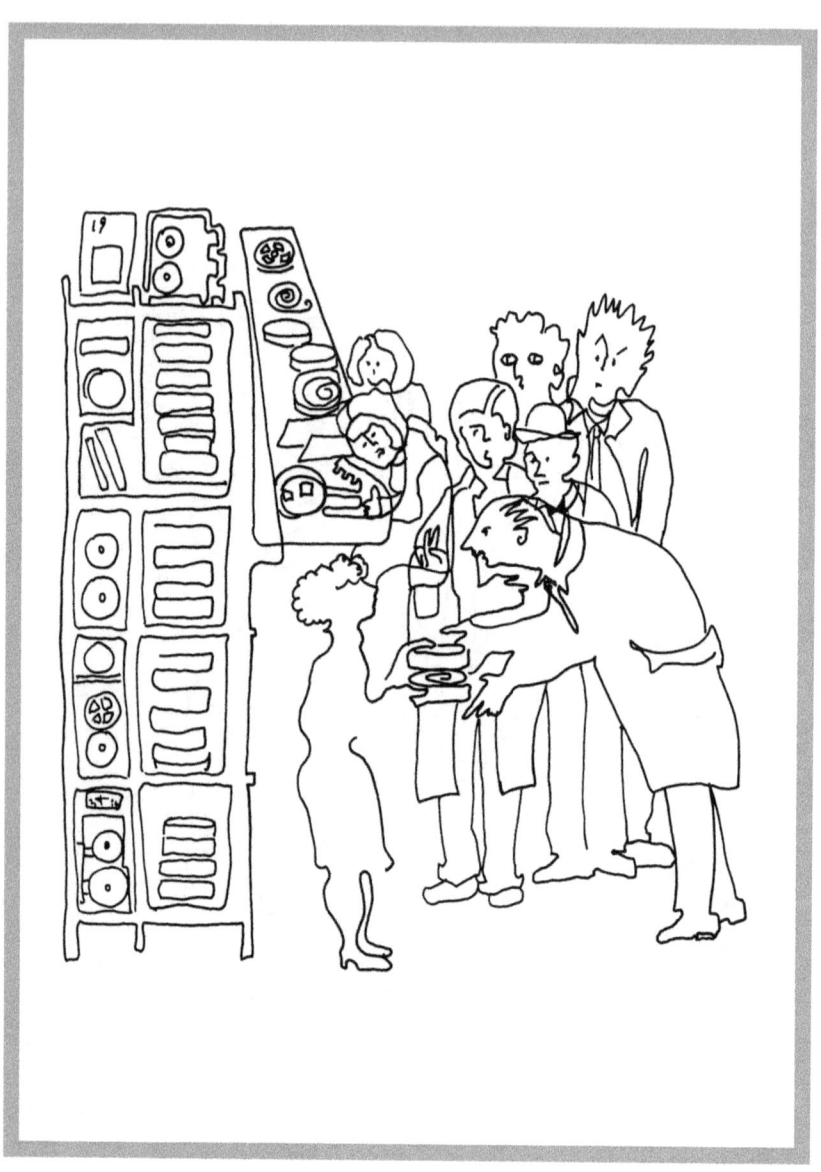

Erinnerungen an eine Labor-Kantine.
Recuerdos de una cantina de laboratorio.
Memories of a laboratory canteen.

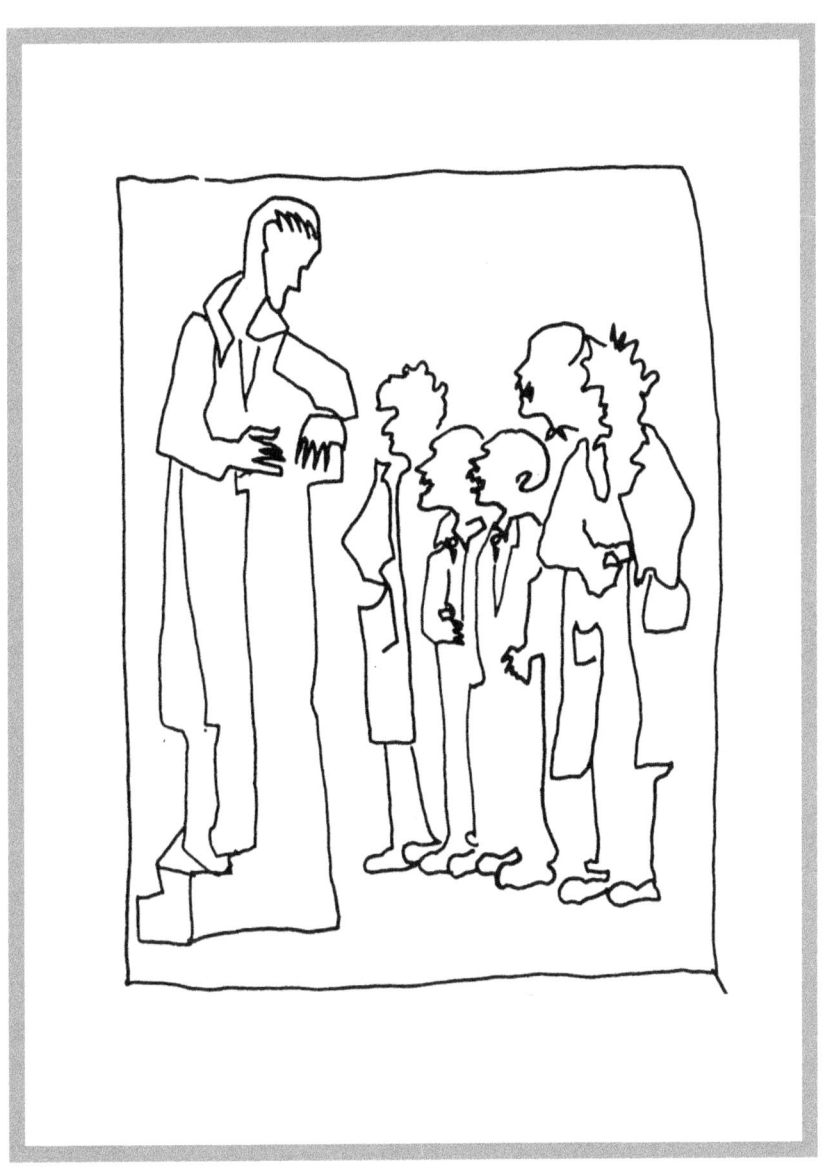

Ein Physiker hält einen Vortrag für Besucher.
Un físico dá una explicación para visitadores.
A physicist gives a talk for visitors.

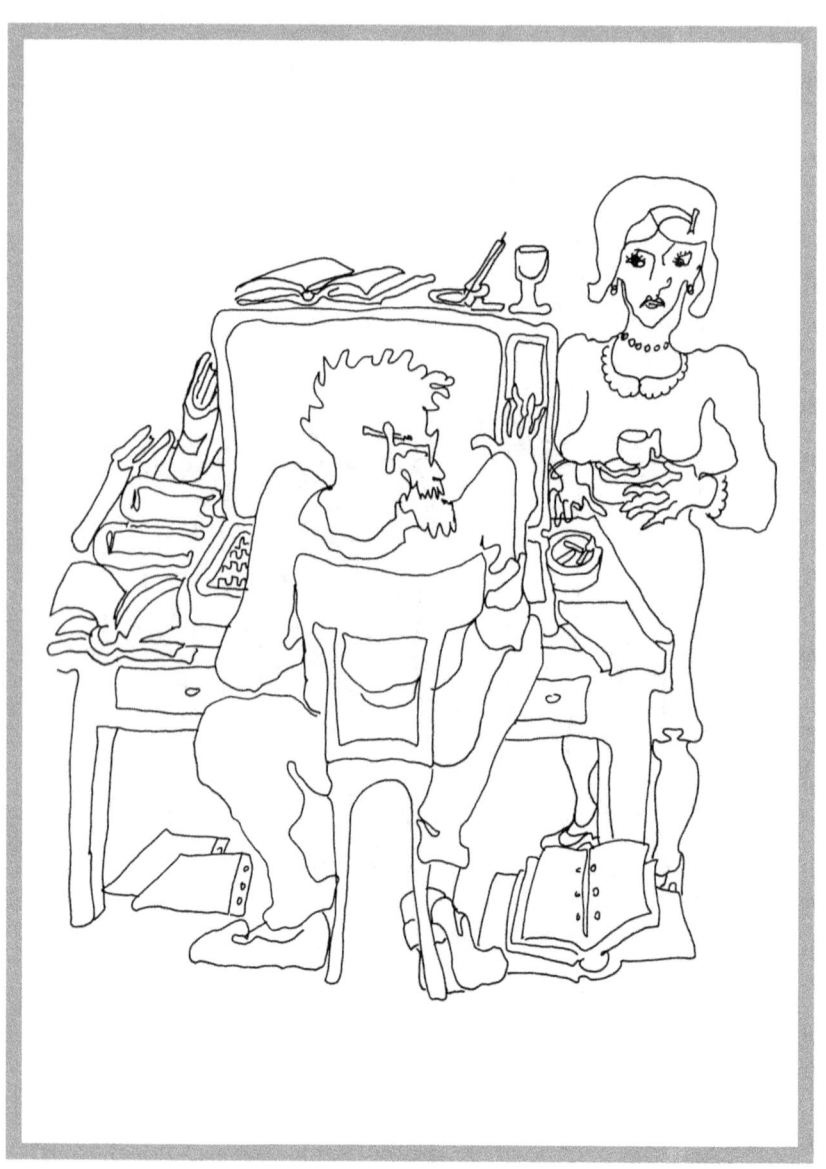

Viele Physiker arbeiten zu Hause weiter.
Muchos físicos siguen trabajando en casa.
Many physicists continue working when they get home.

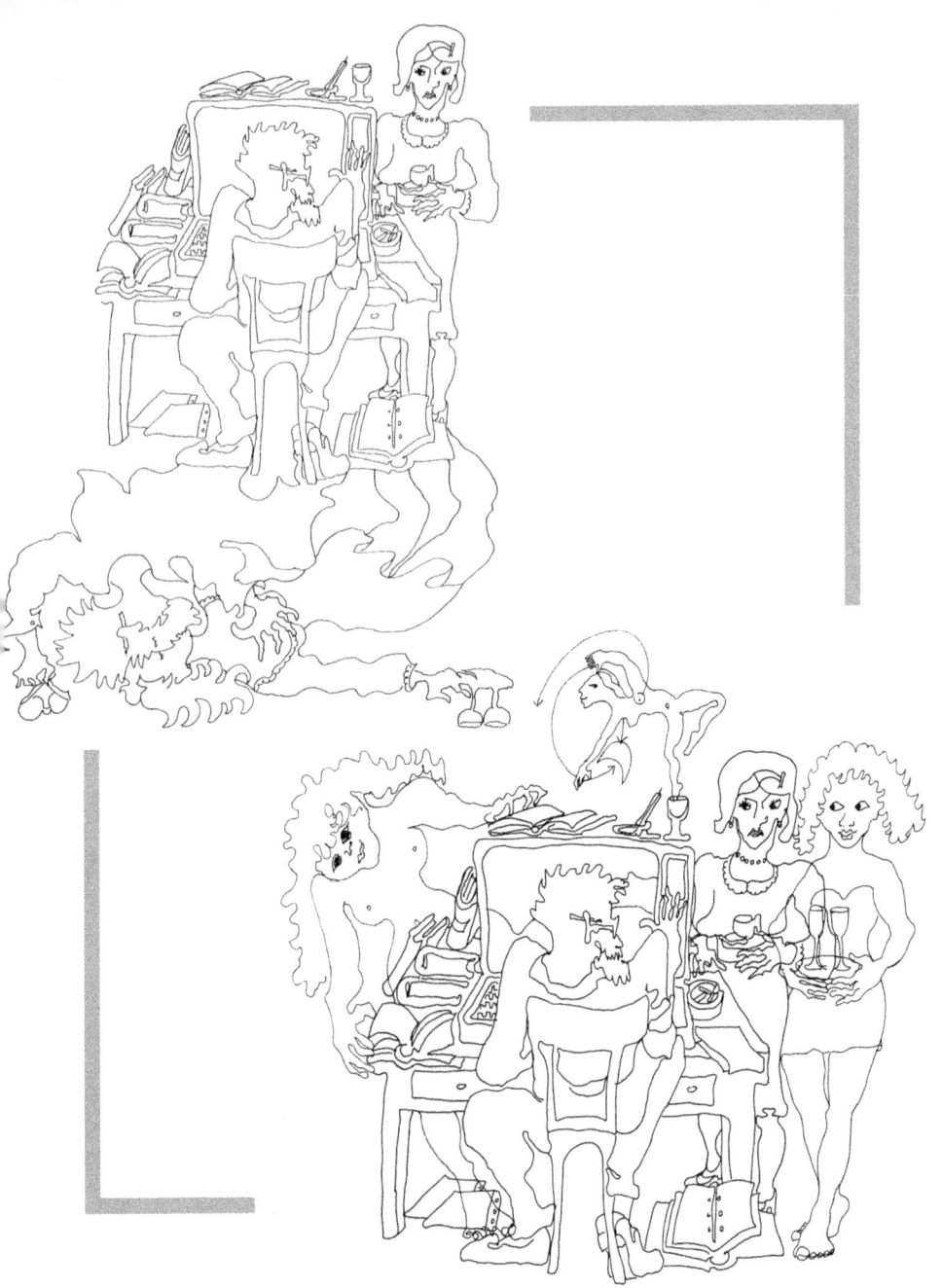

Kein Kommentar.
Sin comentario.
No comment.

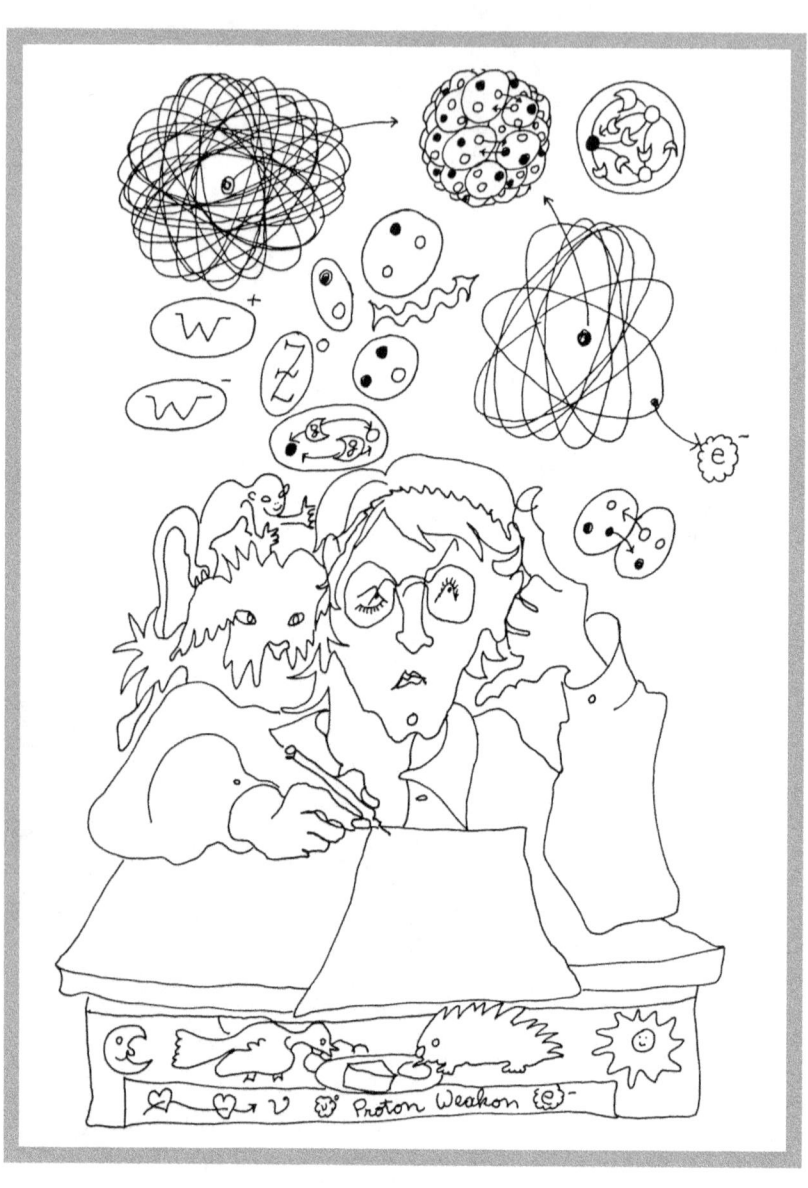

Das Standard-Modell der Teilchenphysik.
El modelo standard de la física de partículas.
The Standard Model of particle physics

Die globalisierten Physiker
Viele Köpfe und viele Hände, ein Ziel.

Los físicos globalizados
Muchas cabezas y muchas manos, una meta.

The Globalized Physicists
Many heads and many hands, one goal.

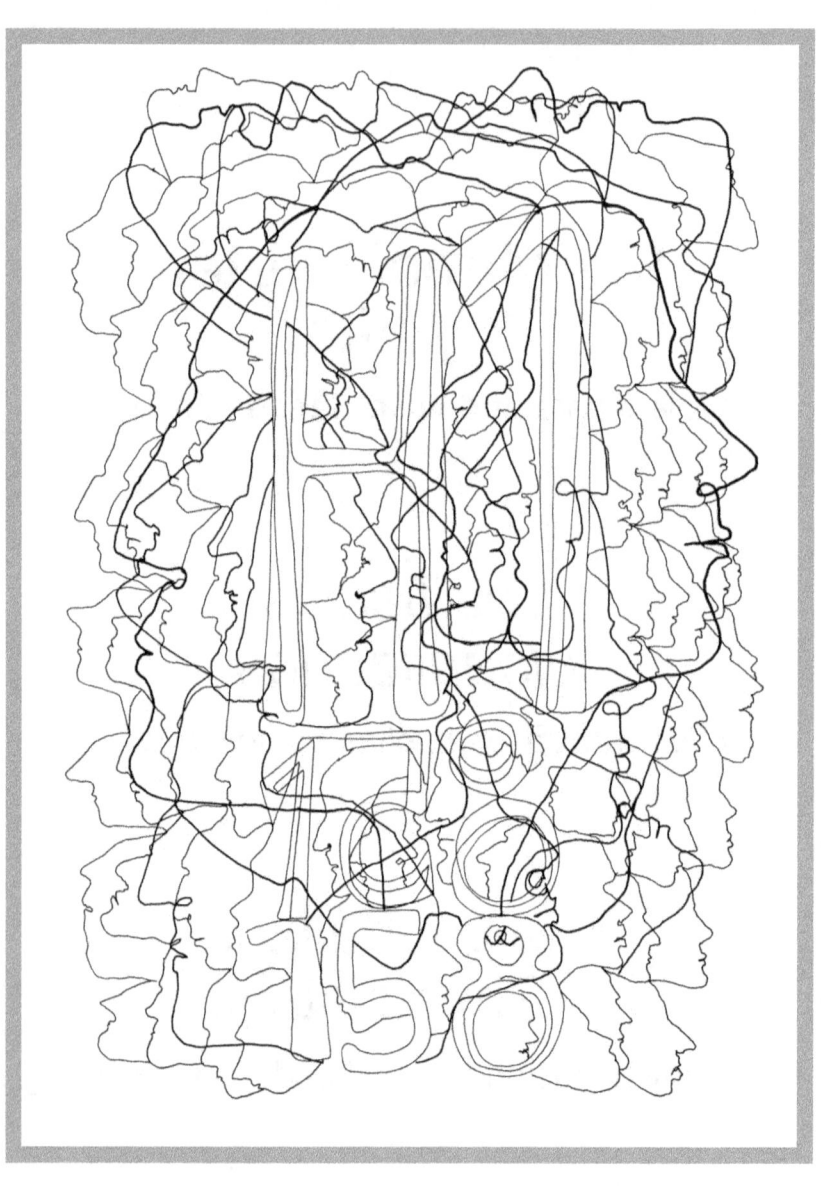

Pedro ist Mitglied Nr. 158 der H1-Kollaboration.
Pedro es miembro Nr. 158 de la colaboración H1.
Pedro is member Nr 158 of the H1 Collaboration.
DESY, 1985

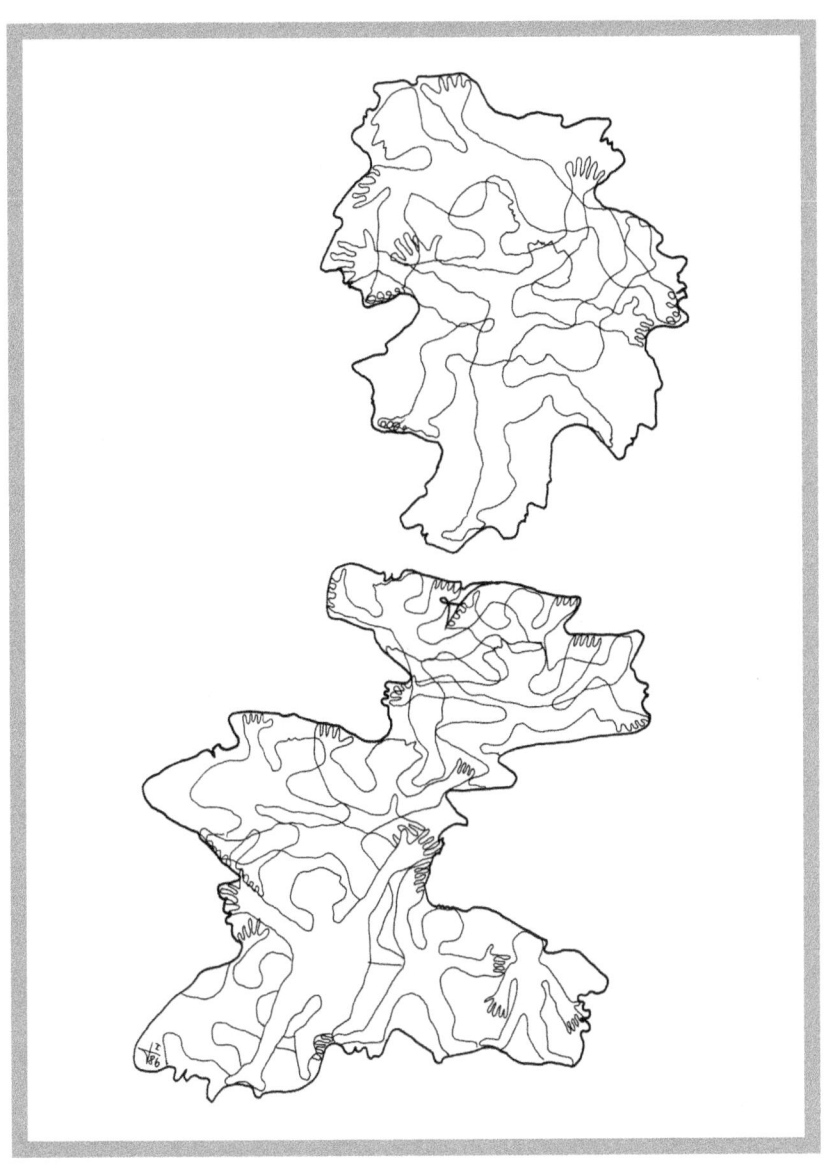

Kleinere Gruppen vereinigen sich.
Grupos pequeños se juntan.
Smaller groups join together.

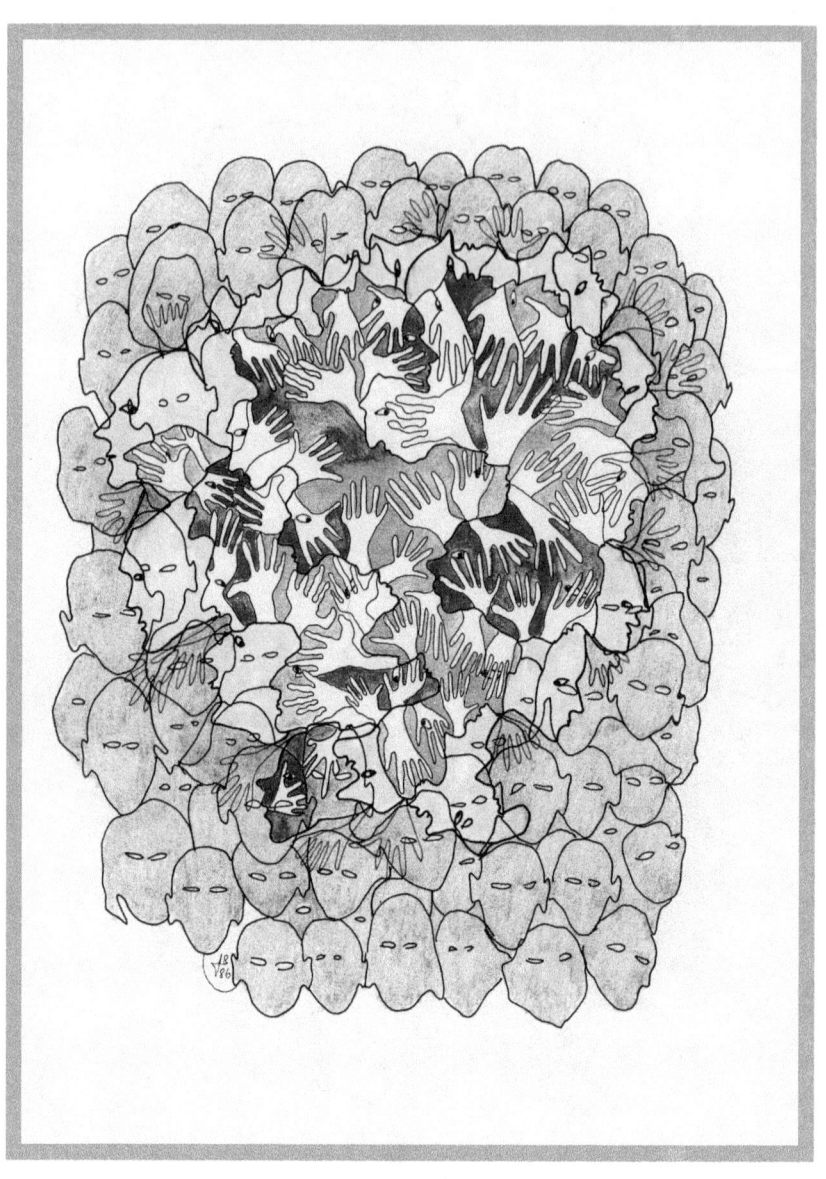

Köpfe und Hände die zusammenhalten.
Cabezas y manos reunidas.
Joining heads and hands.

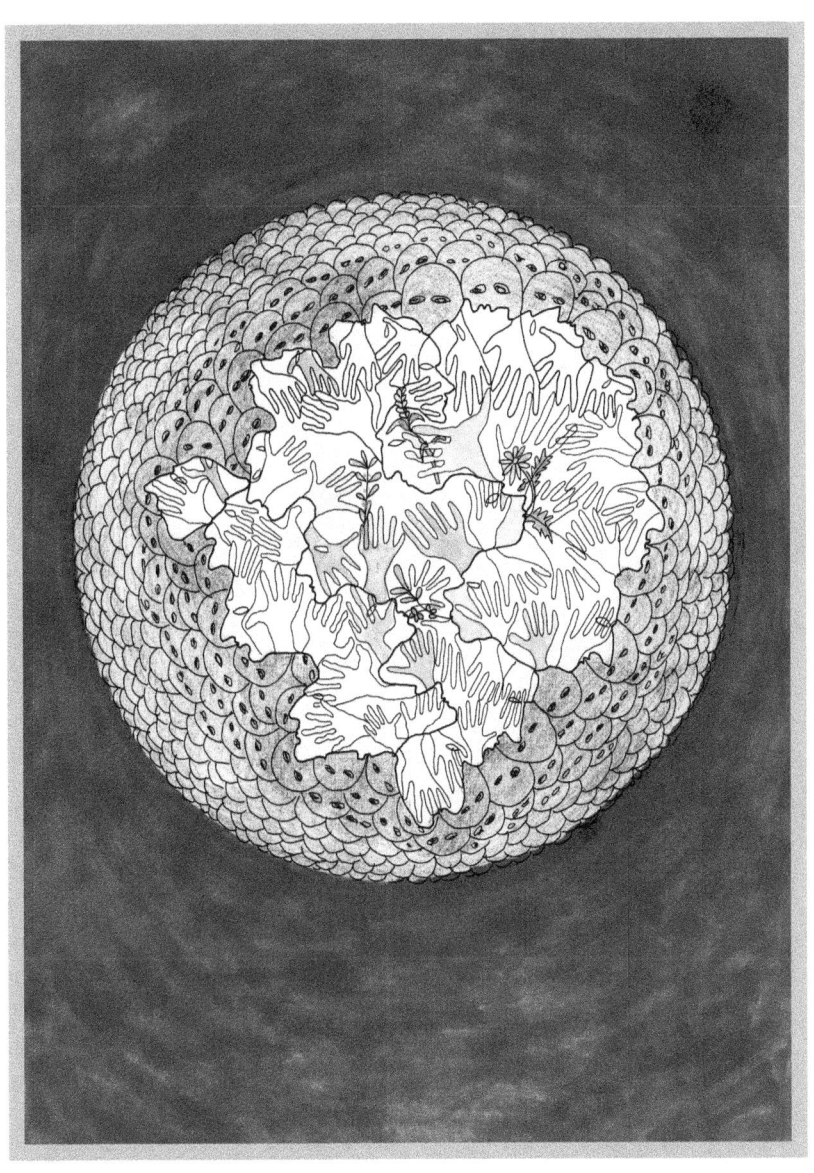

Weltweite Globalisierung der Köpfe und Hände.
Globalización mundial de cabezas y manos.
Worldwide globalization of heads and hands.

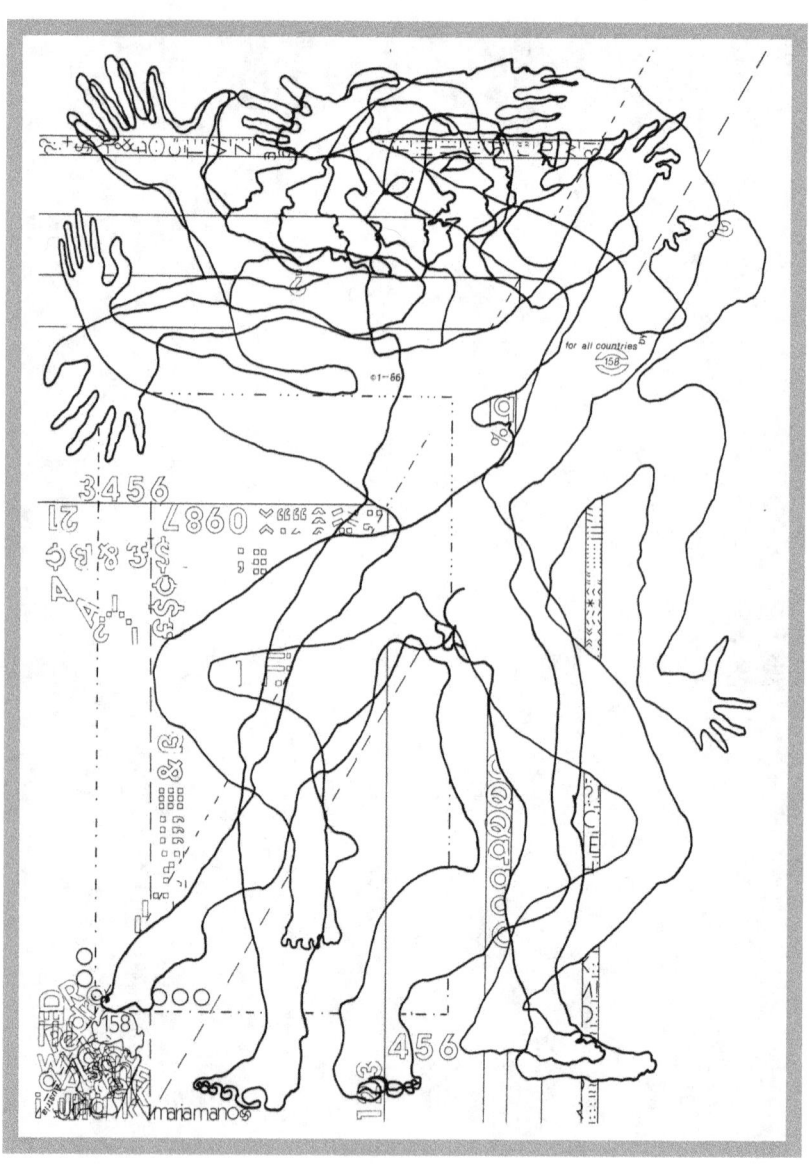

Die Kraft der Zusammenarbeit.
La fuerza de la colaboración.
The power of collaboration.

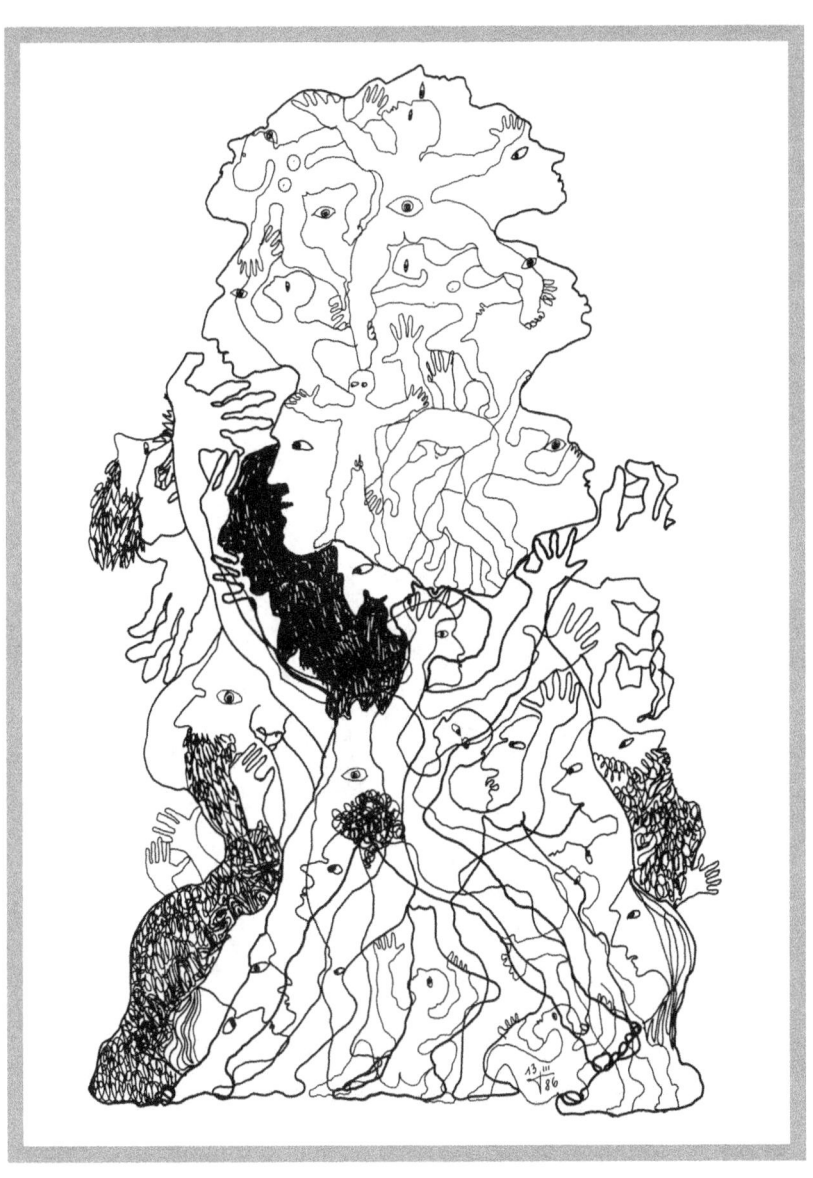

Pyramide der Körper und Hände.
Pirámide de cuerpos y manos.
Pyramid of bodies and hands.

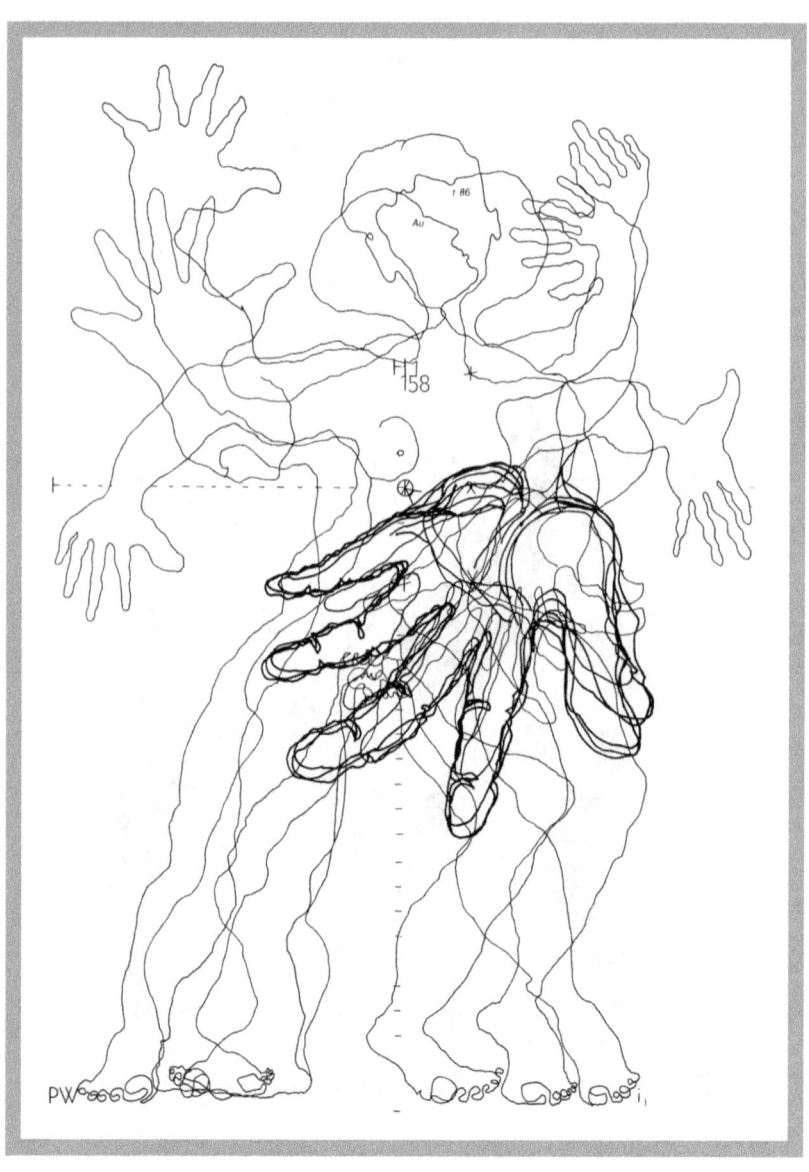

Vereinte Körper und wegweisende Hand.
Cuerpos unidos y mano que guía.
United bodies and guiding hand.

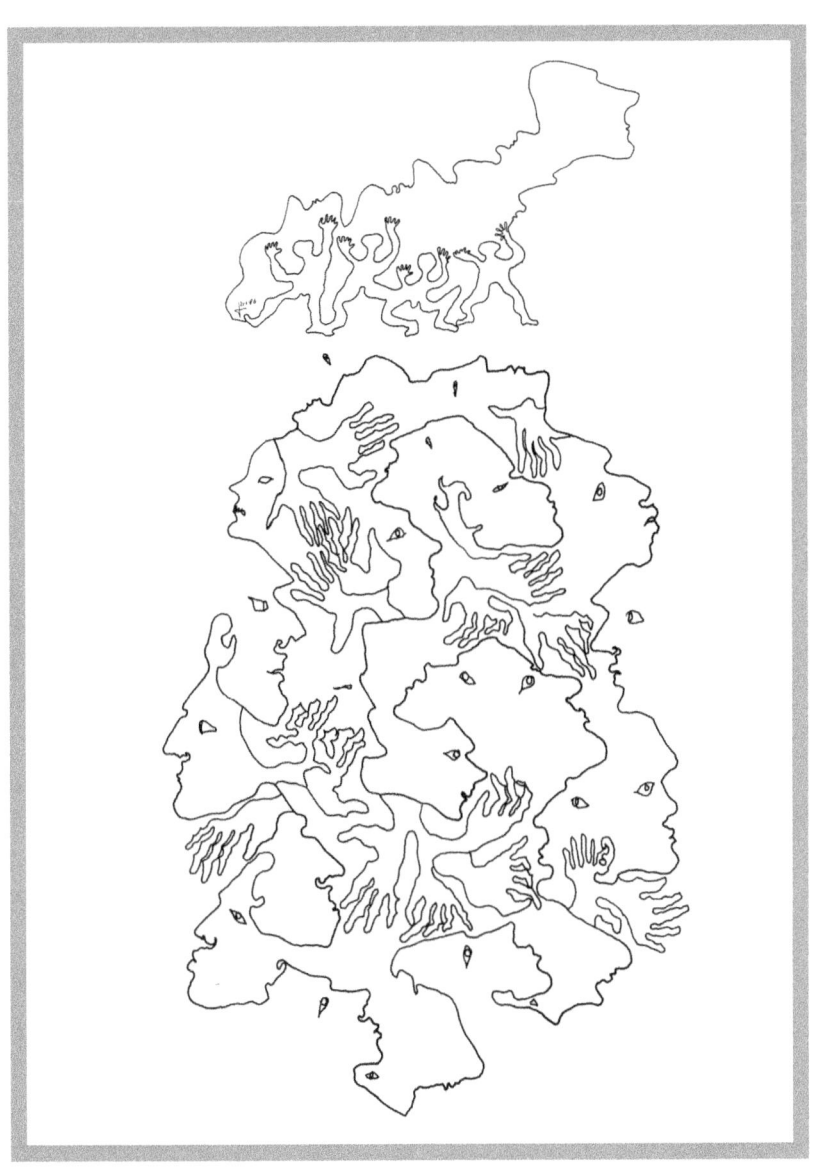

Gesichter und Hände. Oben: Der Gruppensprecher.
Caras y manos. Arriba: el portavoz del grupo.
Faces and hands. Above: the group's speaker.

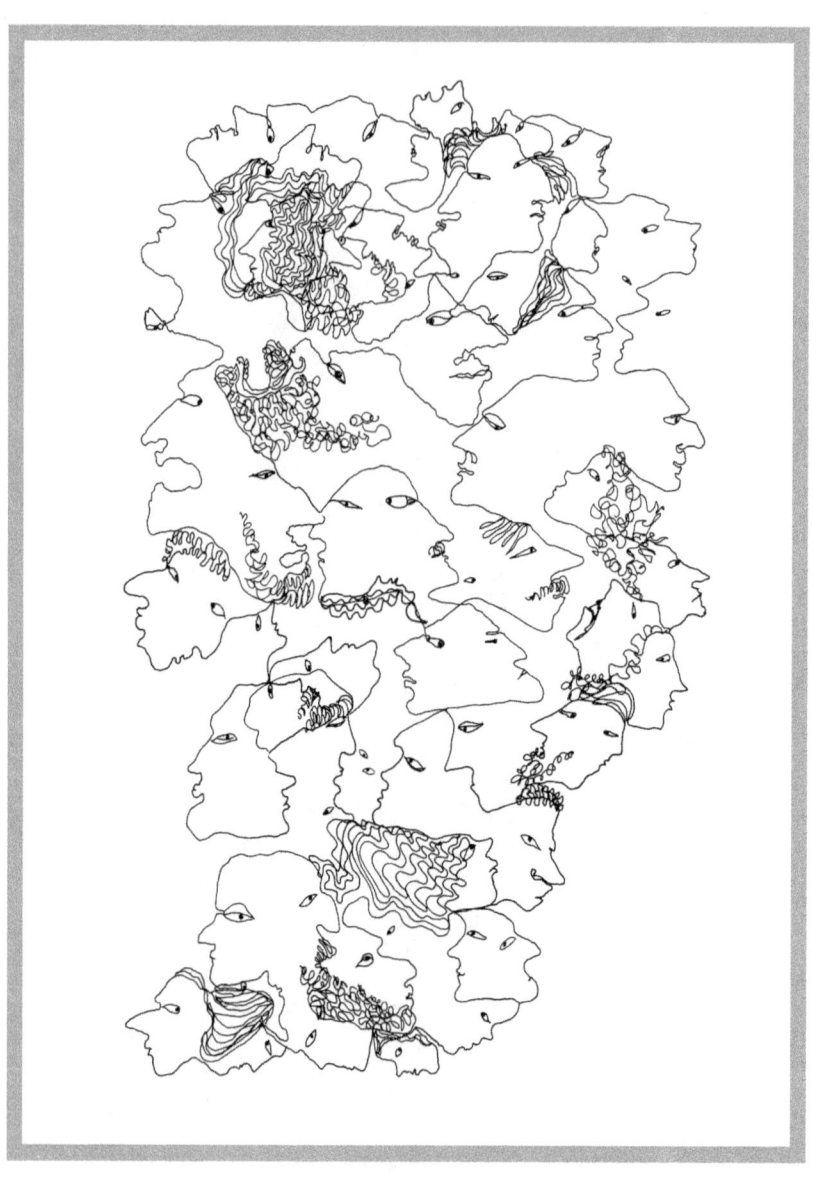

Vereinte Gesichter.
Caras unidas.
United faces.

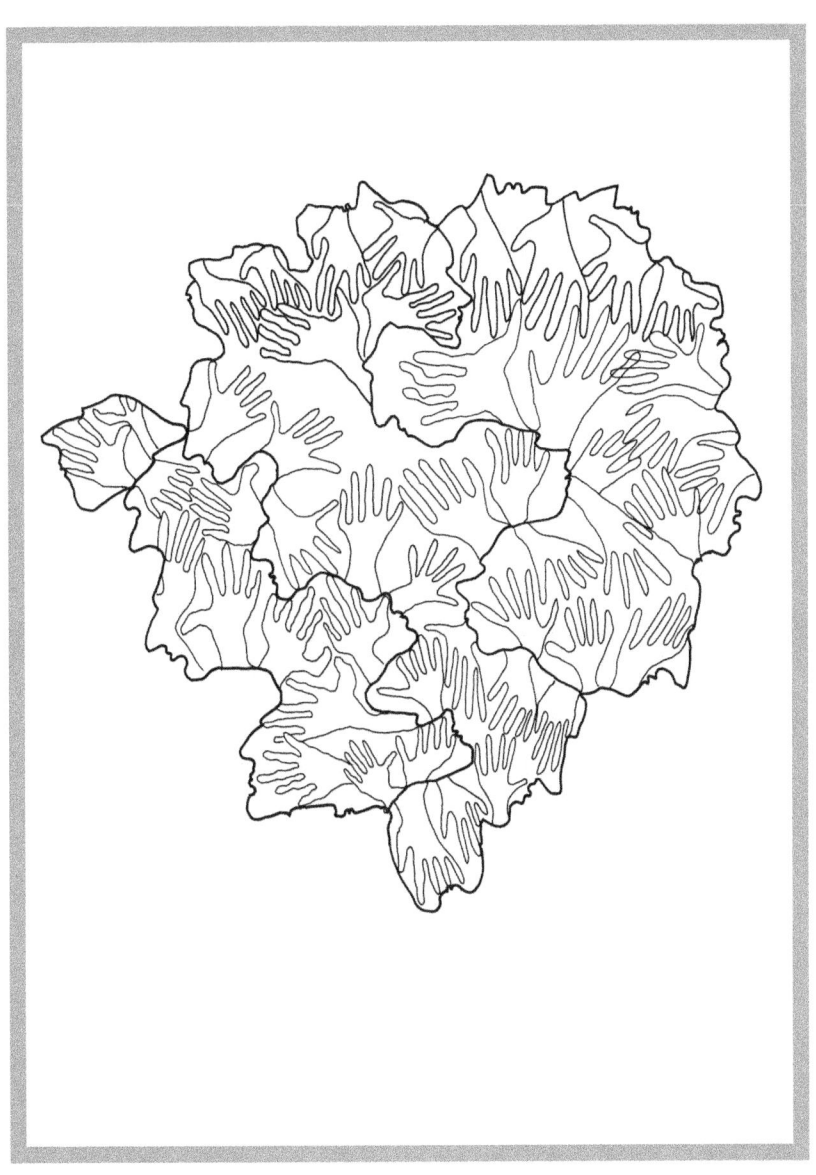

Vereinte Hände.
Manos unidas.
United hands.

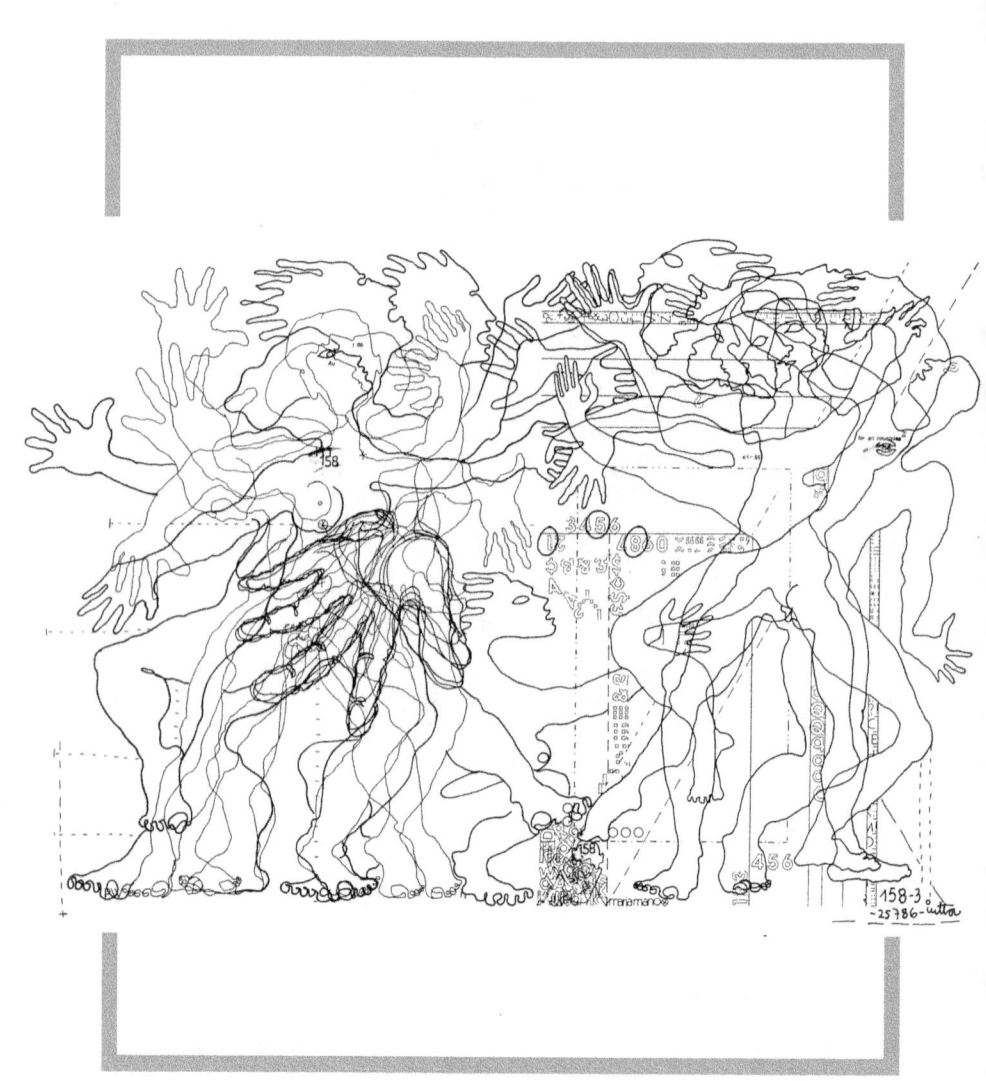

Zusammenstellung.
Composición.
Compilation.

Physikerporträts
Am Computer bearbeitete Zeichnungen
(alphabetisch geordnet)

Retratos de Físicos
Dibujos retocados en la computadora
(en órden alfabético)

Physicists' Portraits
Computer-edited Drawings
(in alphabetic order)

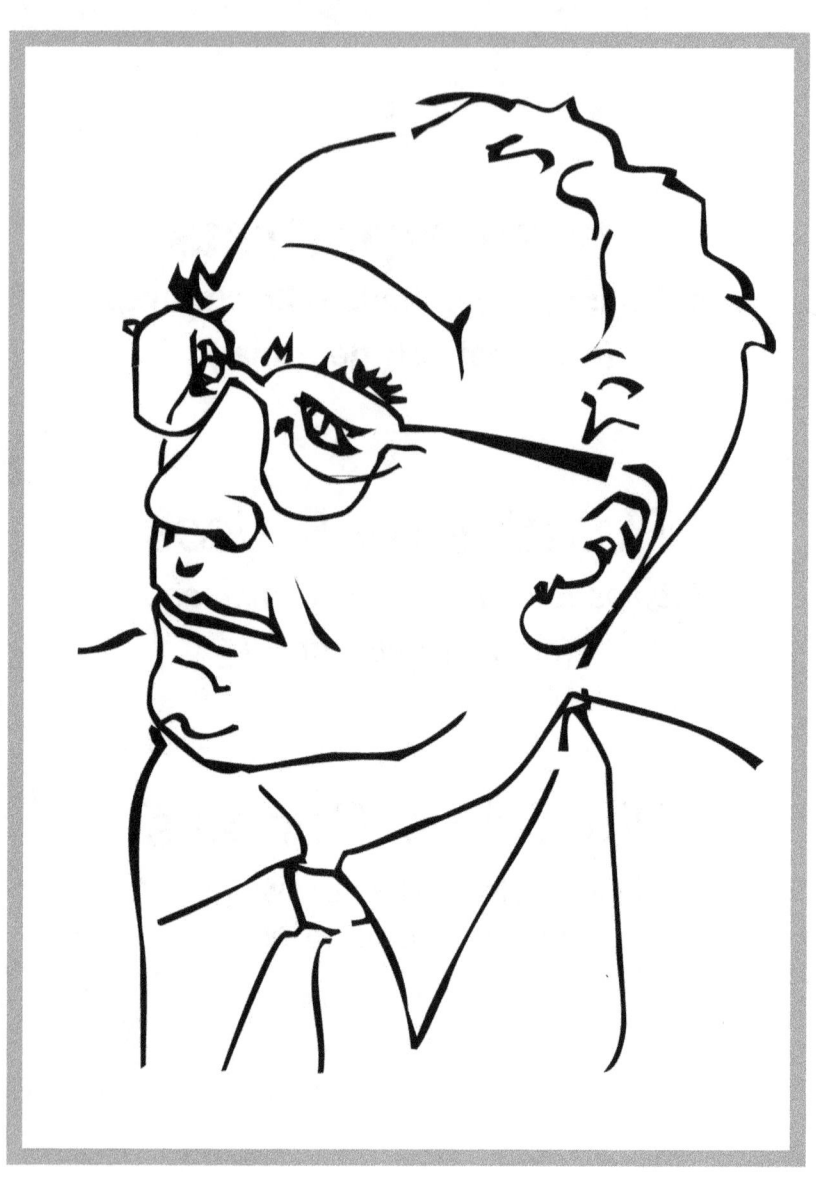

Carl David Anderson (1905-1991)

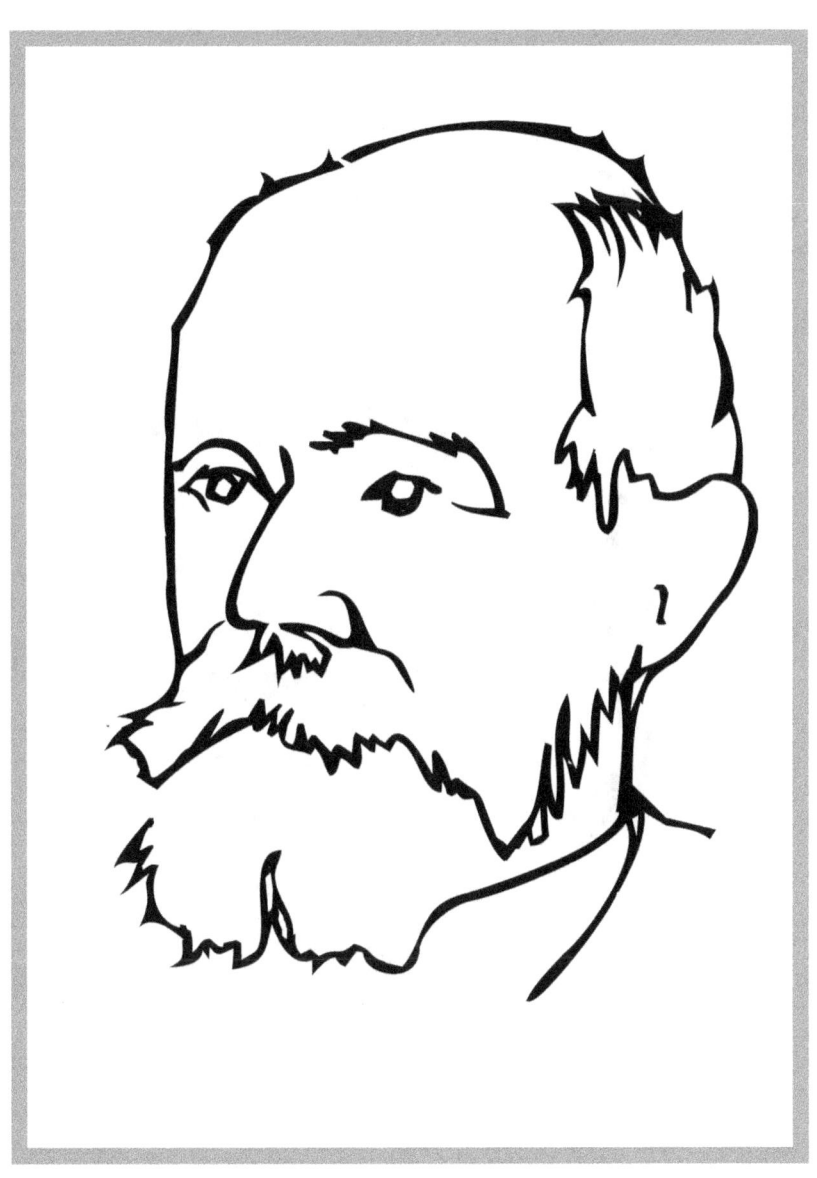

Antoine Henri Becquerel (1852-1908)

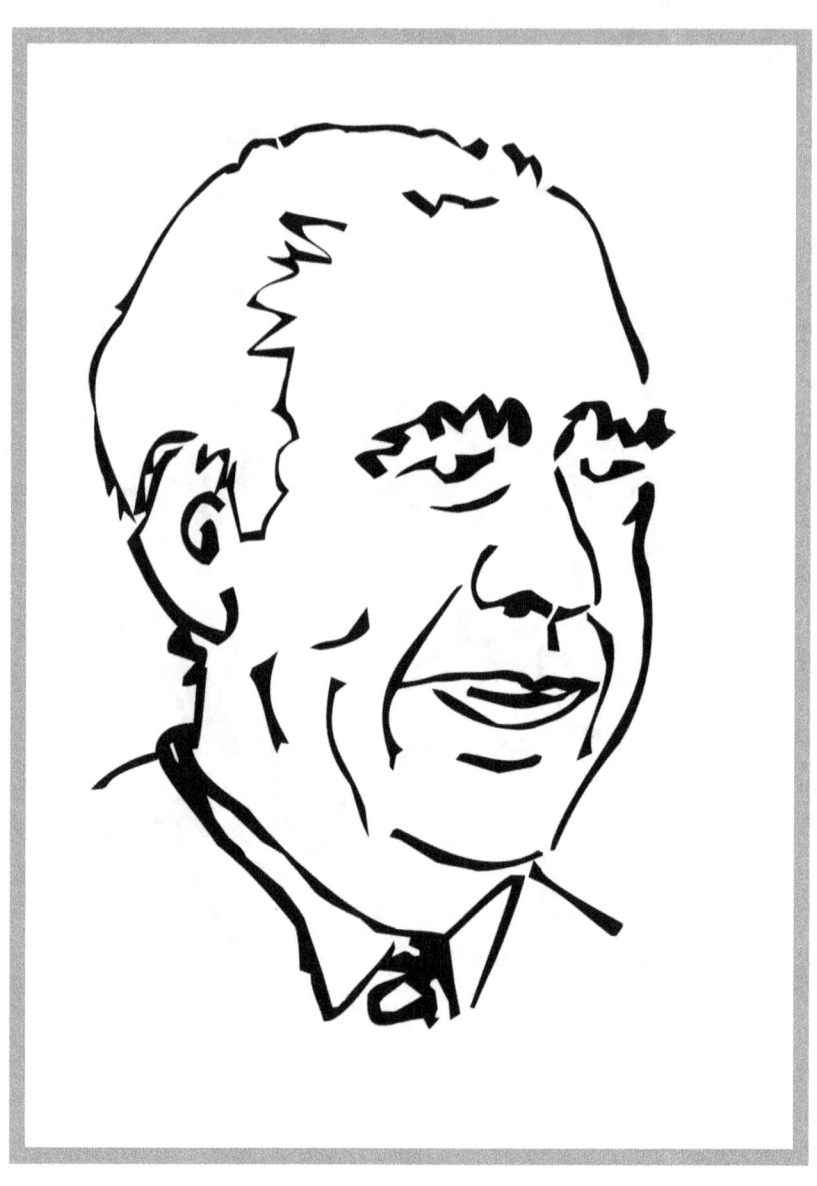

Niels Henrik David Bohr (1885-1962)

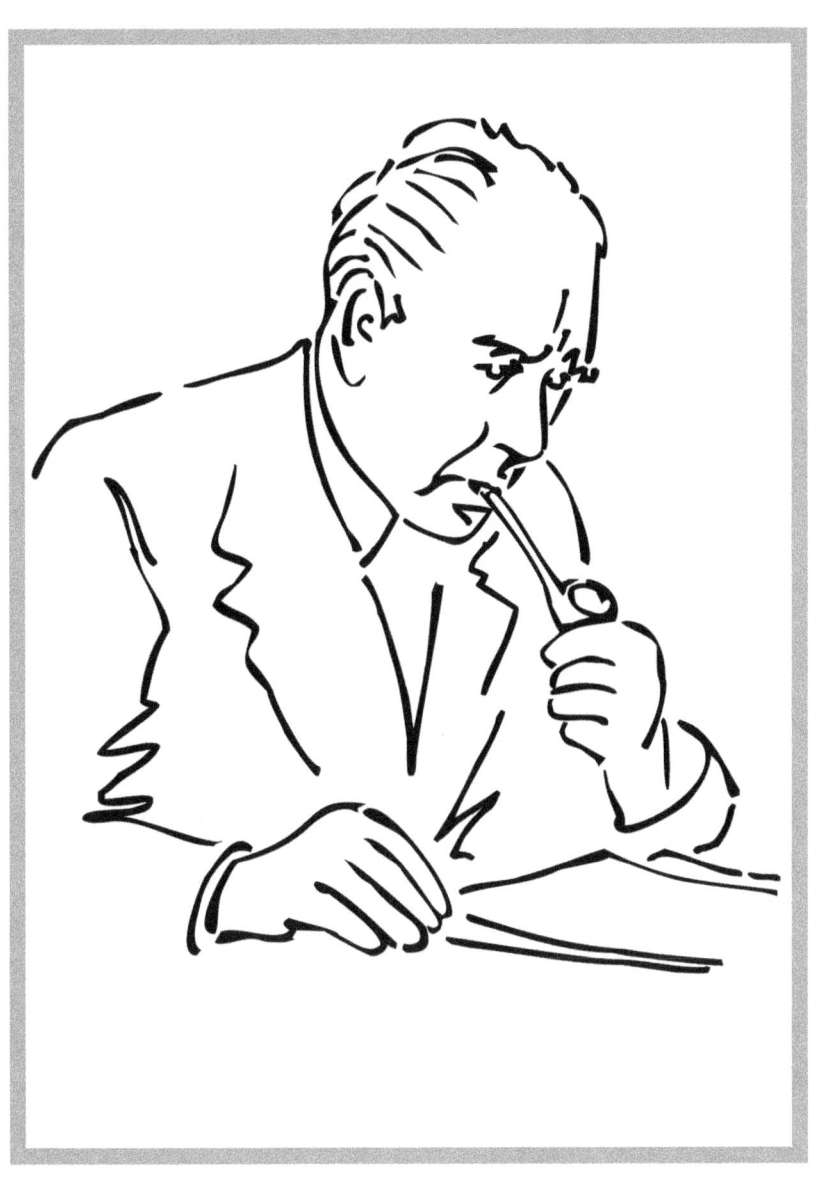

Niels Henrik David Bohr (1885-1962)

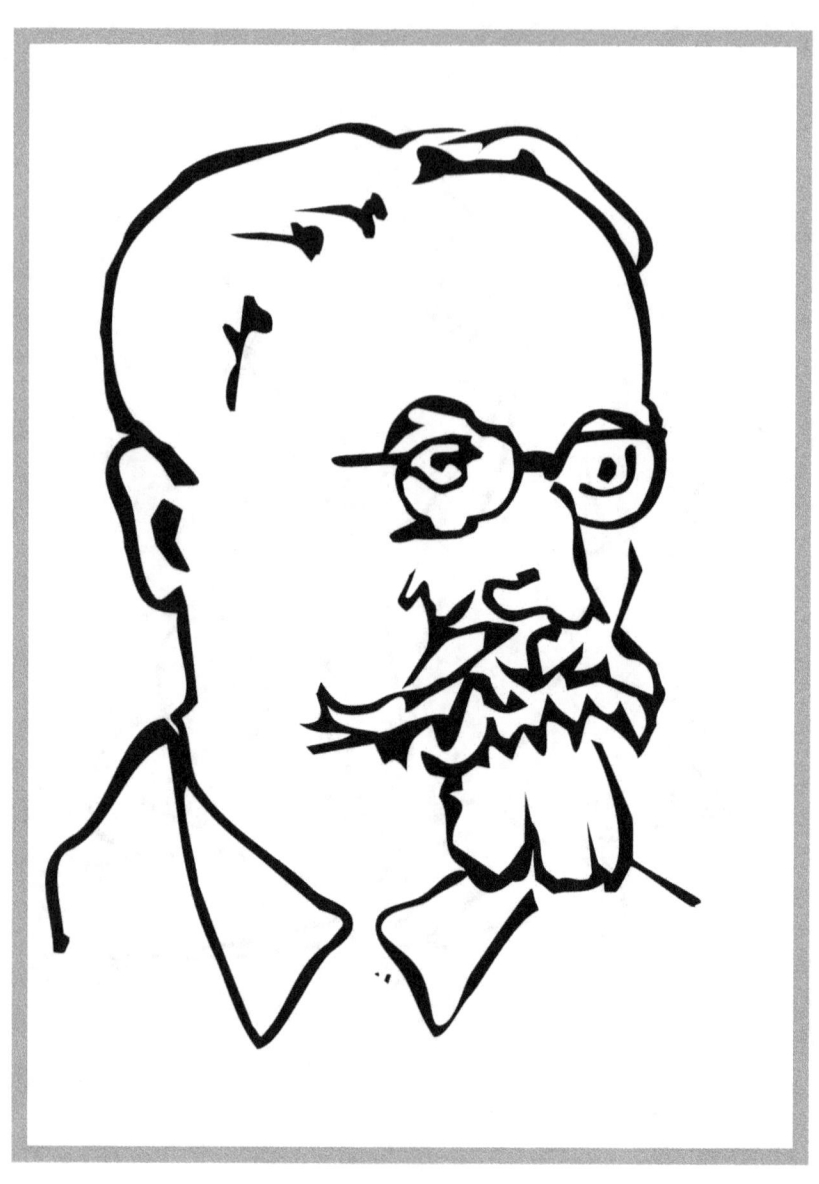

Karl Ferdinand Braun (1850-1918)

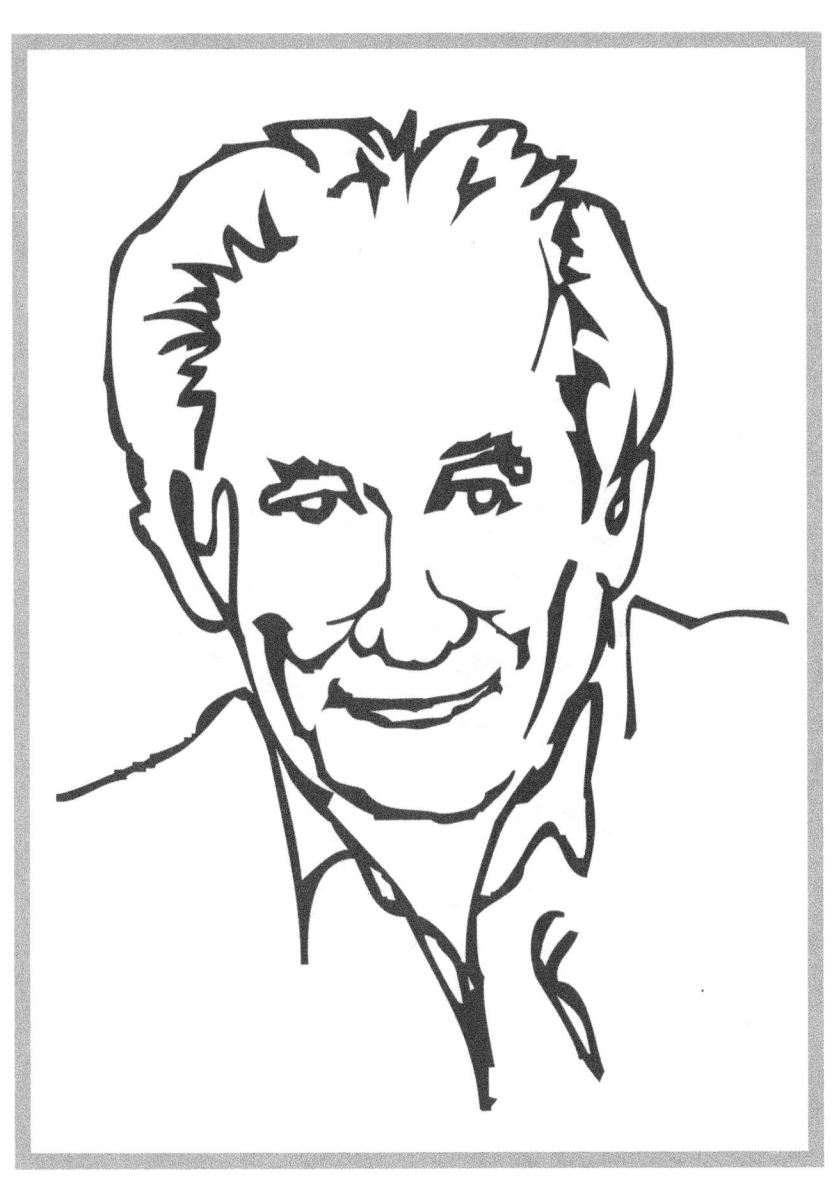

Georges Charpak (1924...)

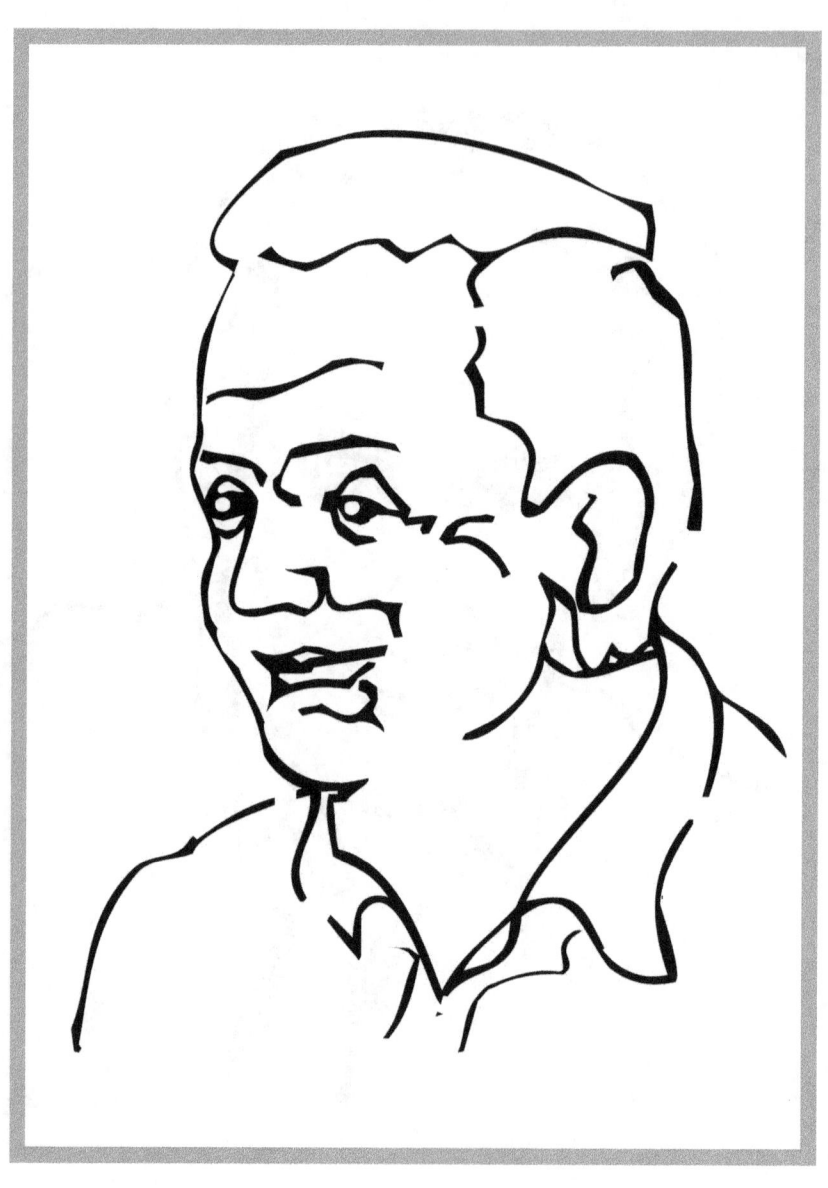

Clyde Lorrain Cowan (1918-1974)

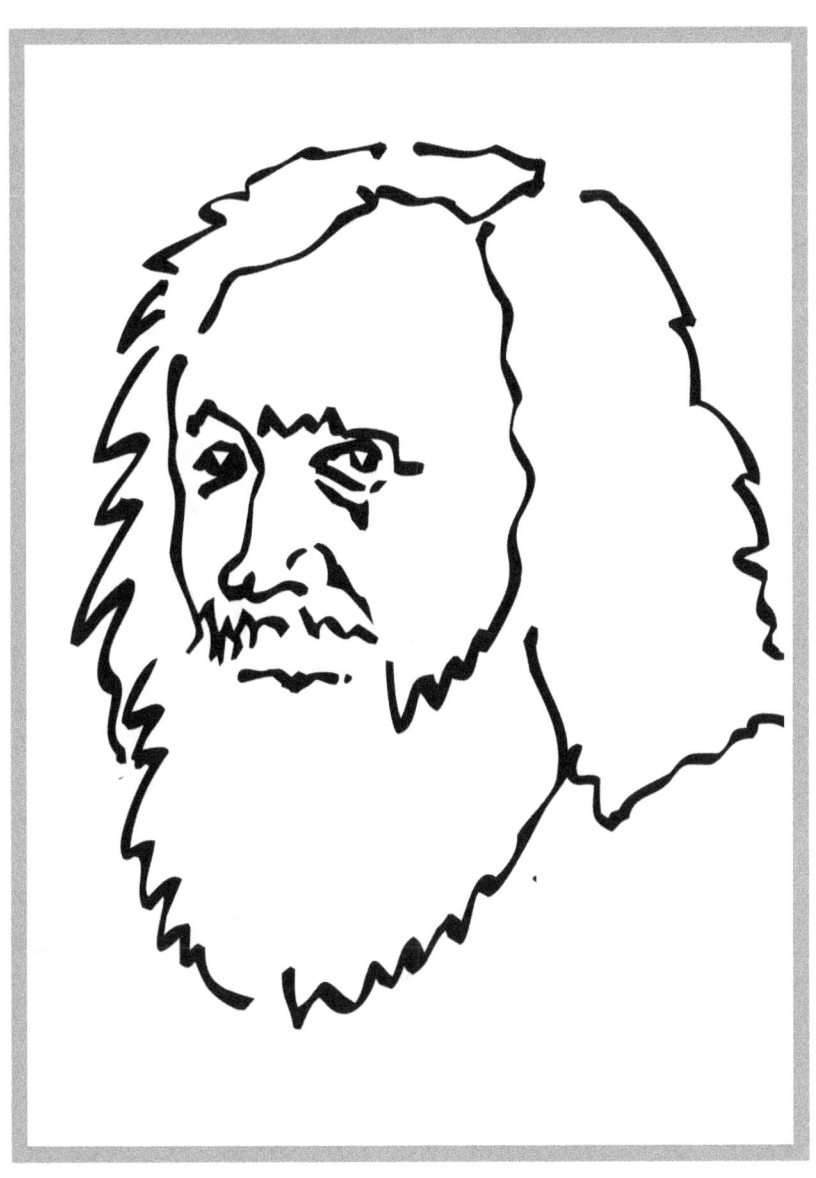

John Dalton (1766-1844)

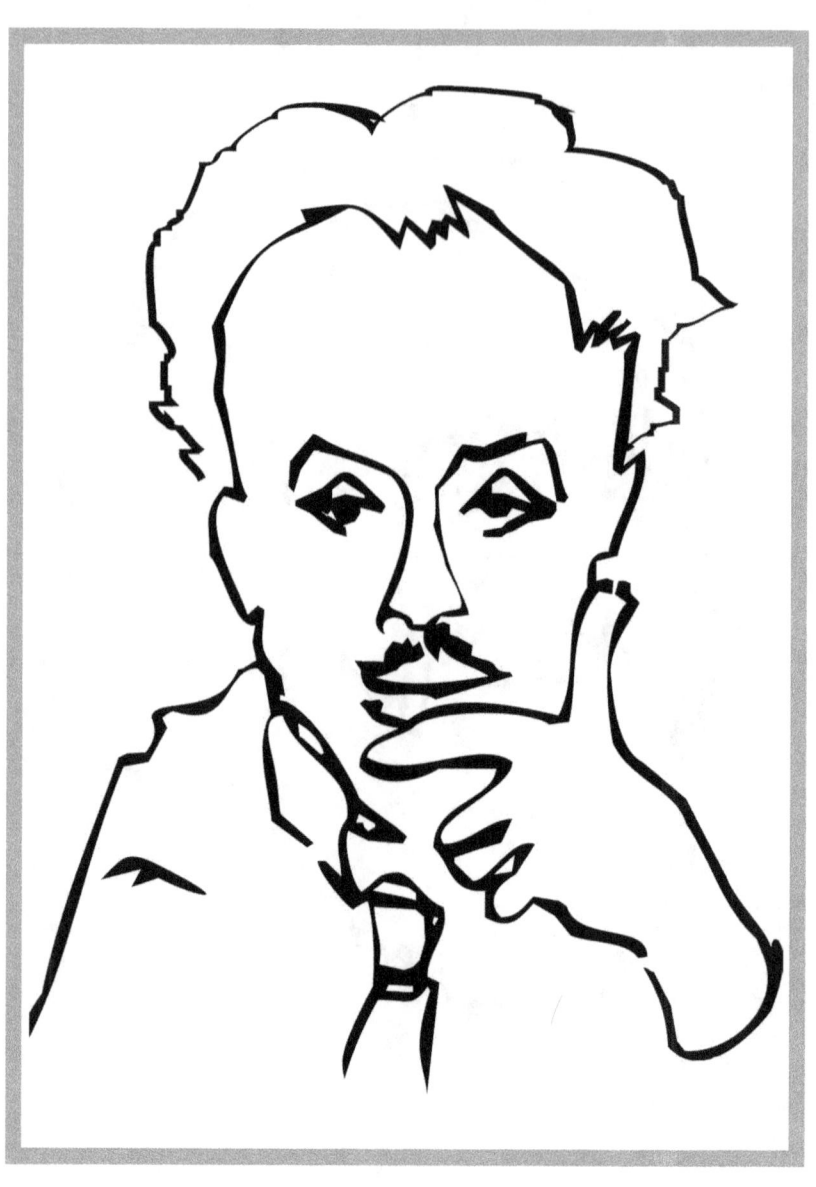

Prince Louis-Victor Pierre Raymond de Broglie
(1892-1987)

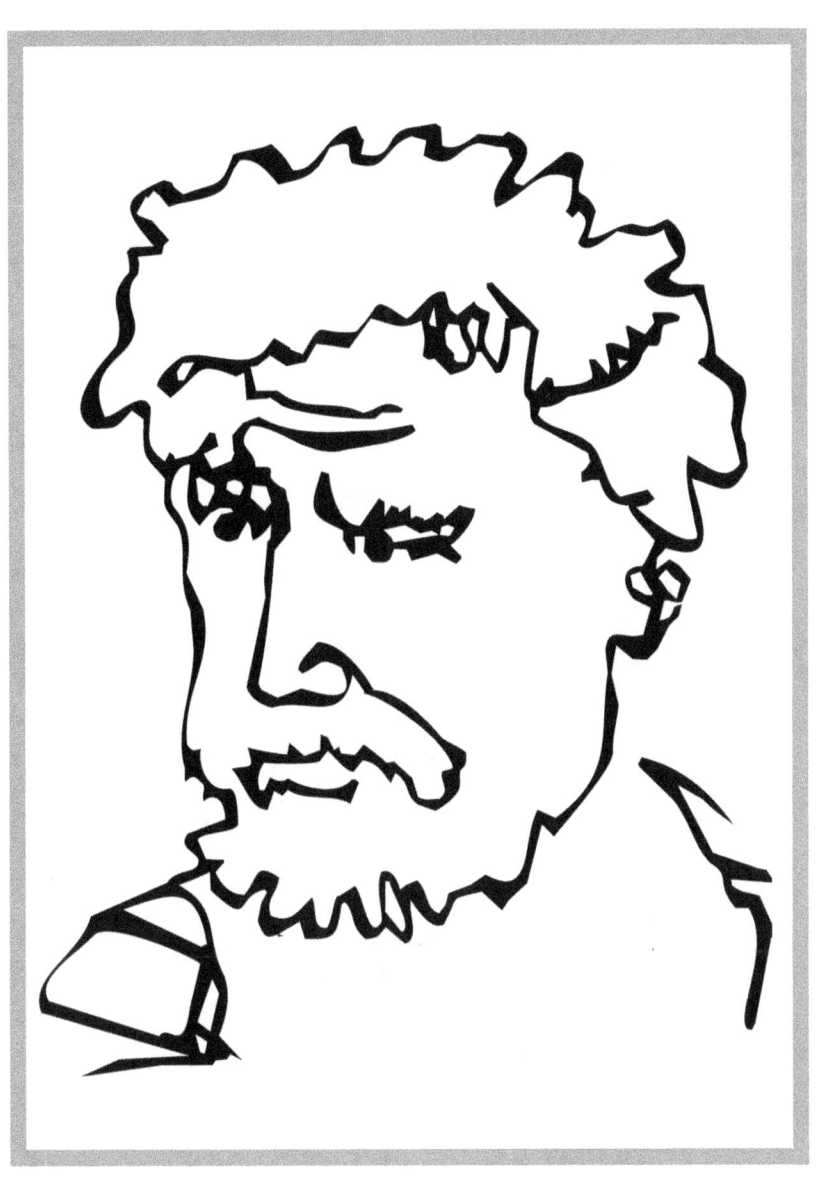

Demokrit (~ 460-370 a.Chr.)

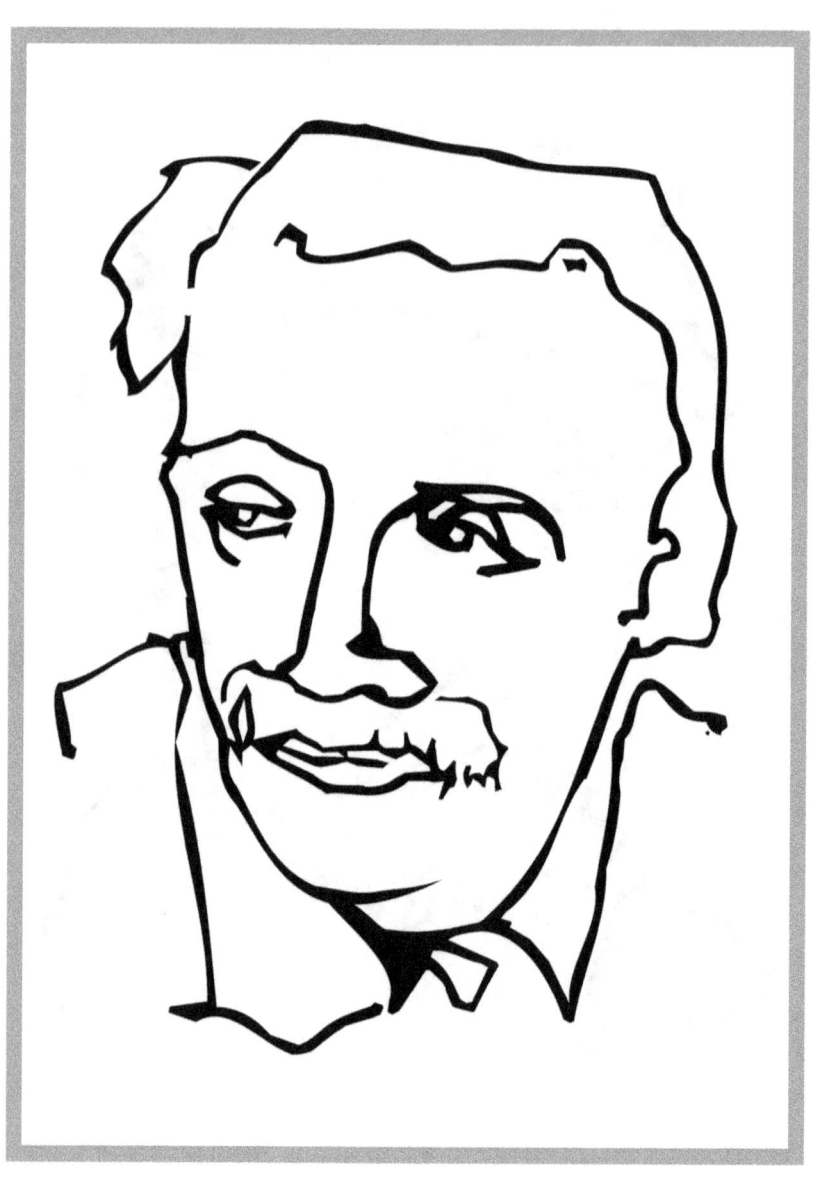

Paul Adrein Maurice Dirac (1902-1984)

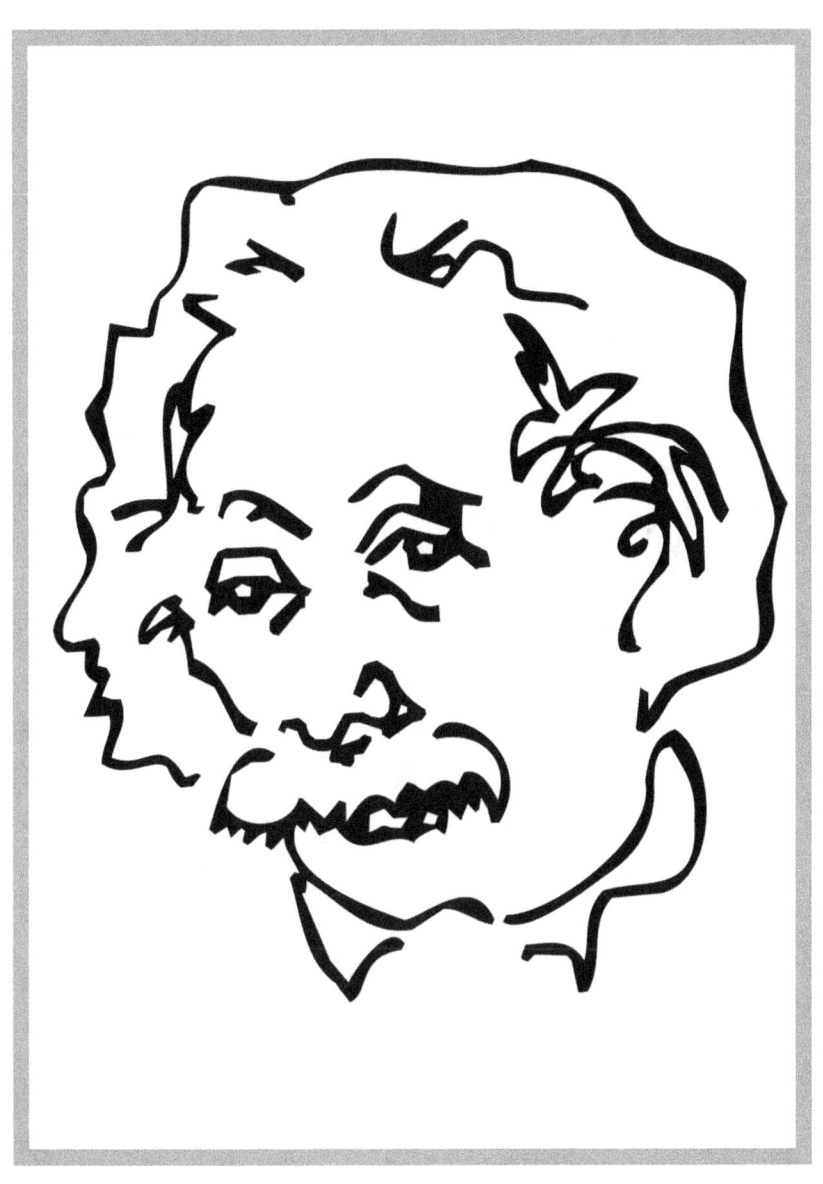

Albert Einstein (1879-1955)

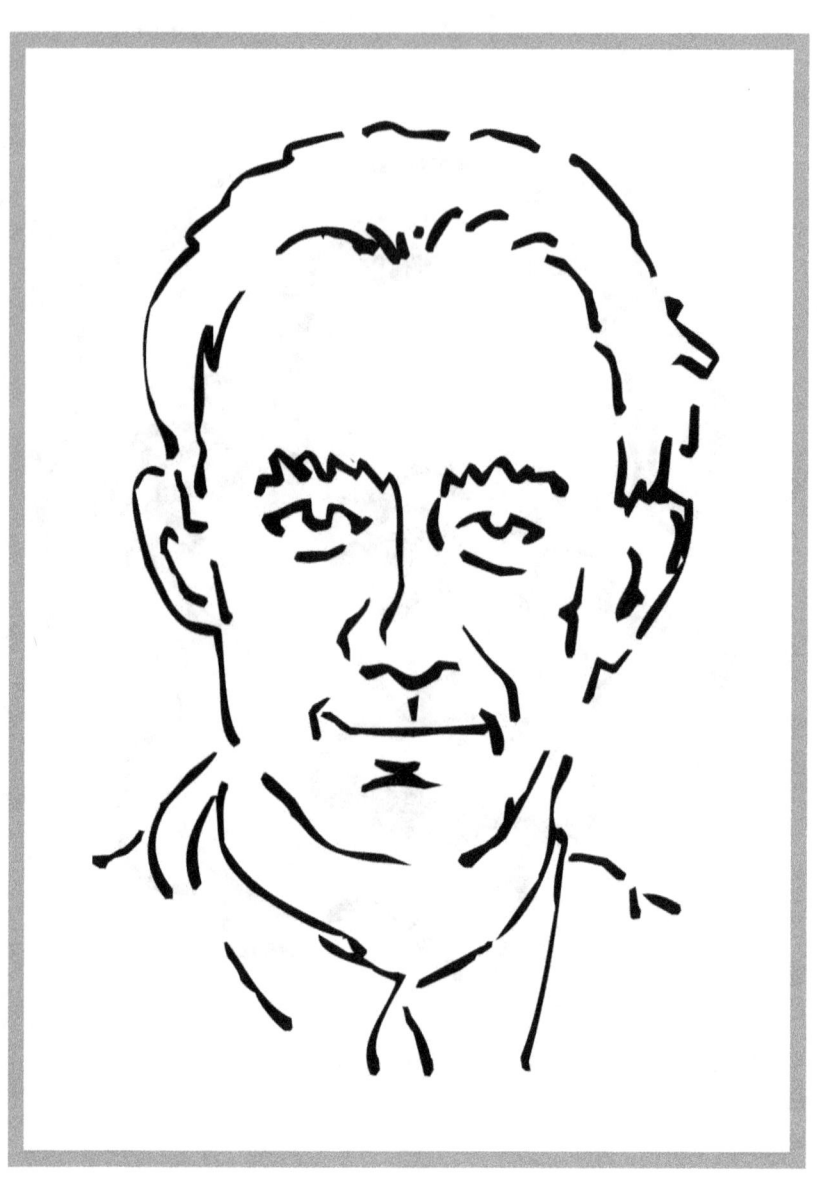

Enrico Fermi (1901-1954)

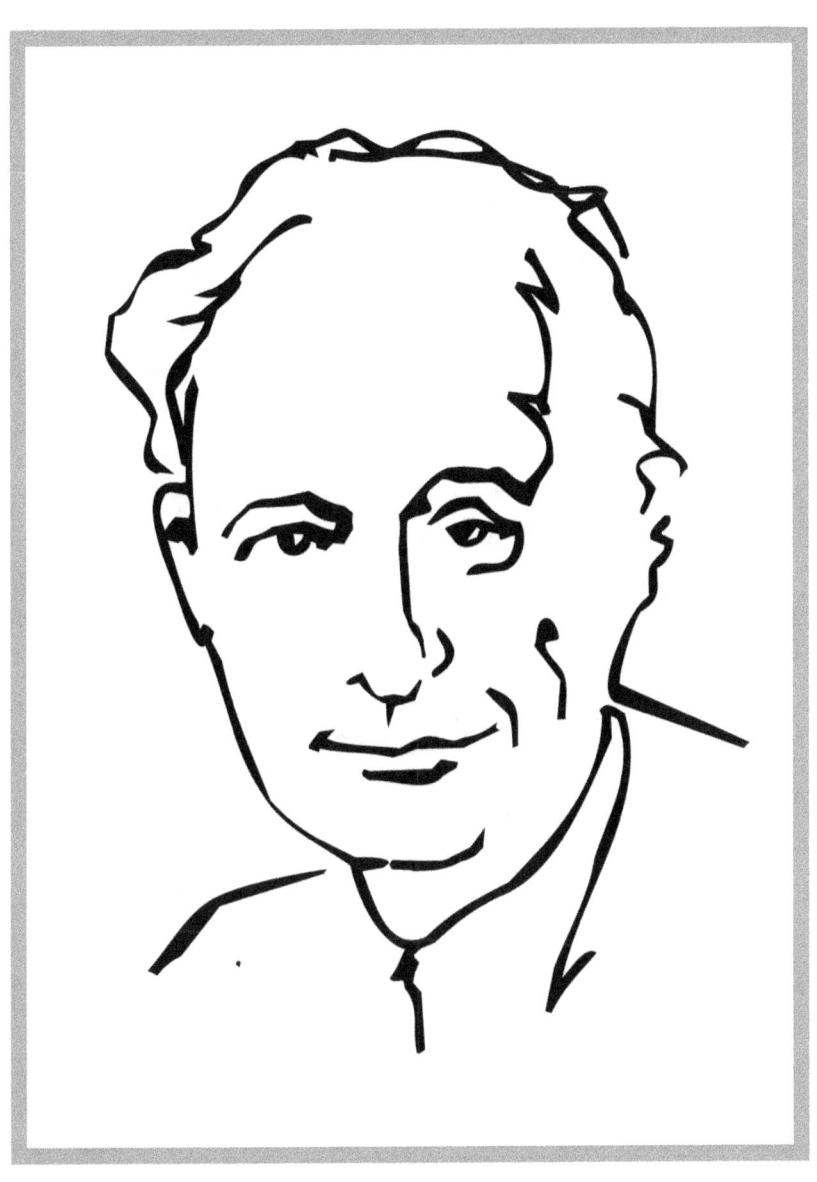

Enrico Fermi (1901-1954)

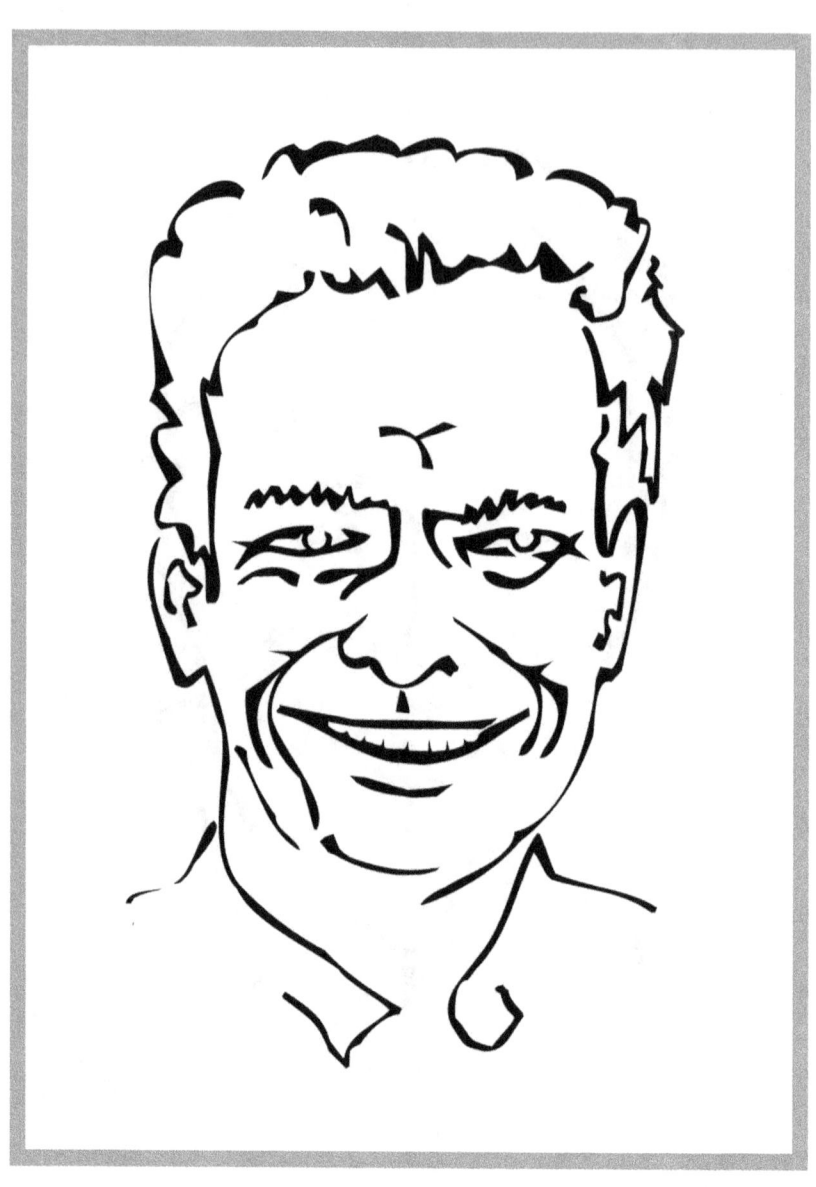

Richard Phillips Feynman (1918-1988)

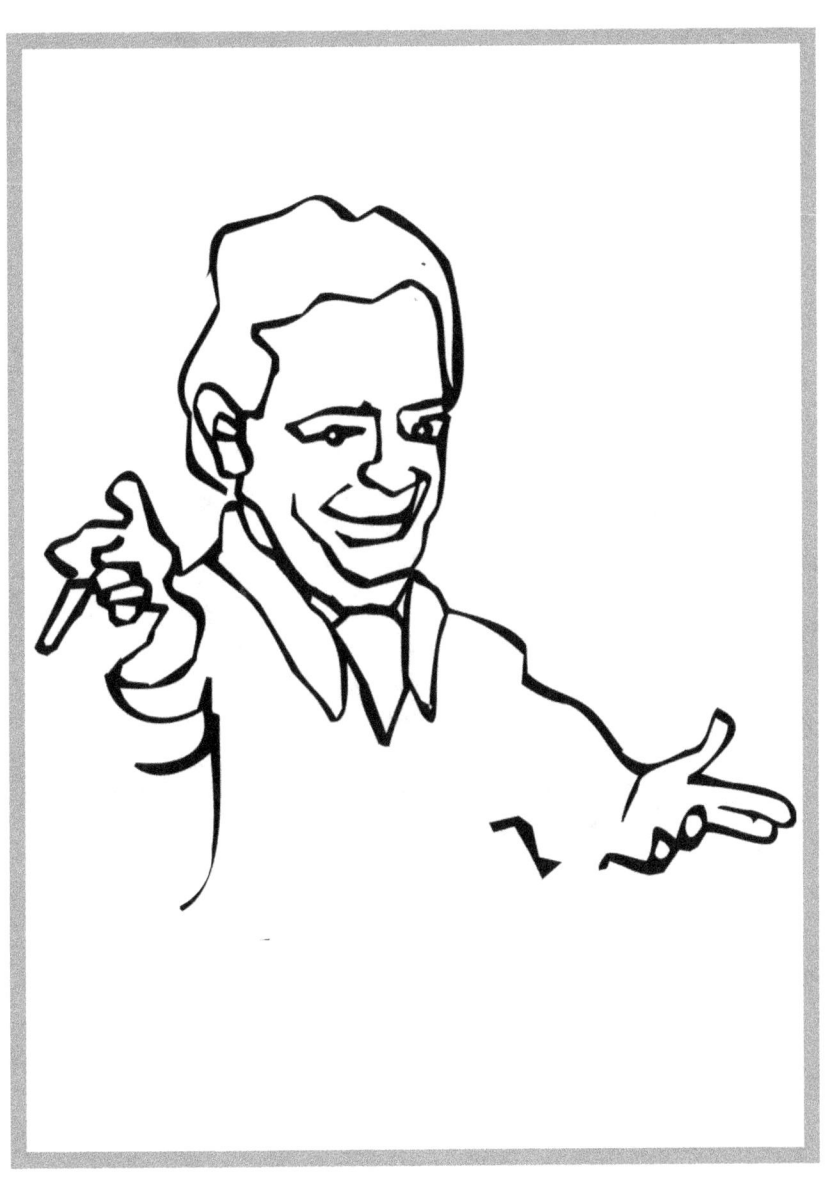

Richard Phillips Feynman (1918-1988)

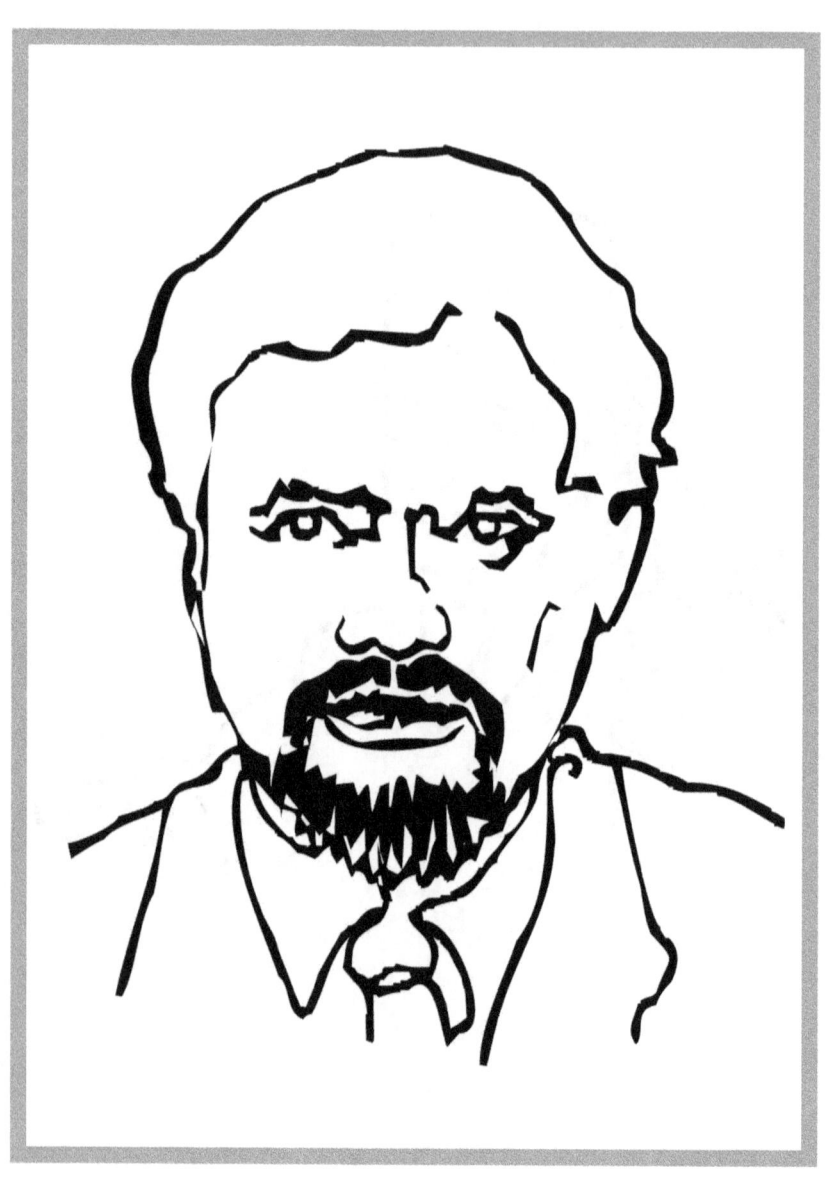

Harald Fritzsch (1943...)

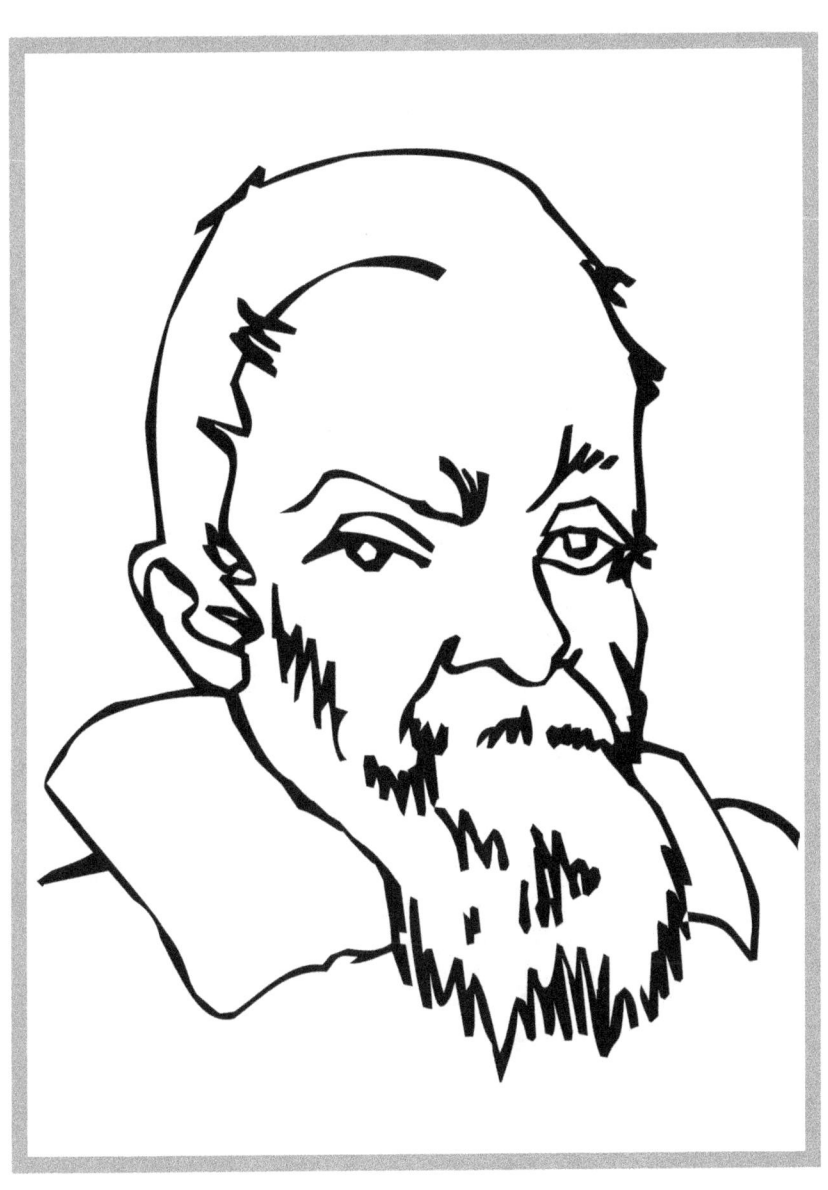

Galileo Galilei (1564-1642)

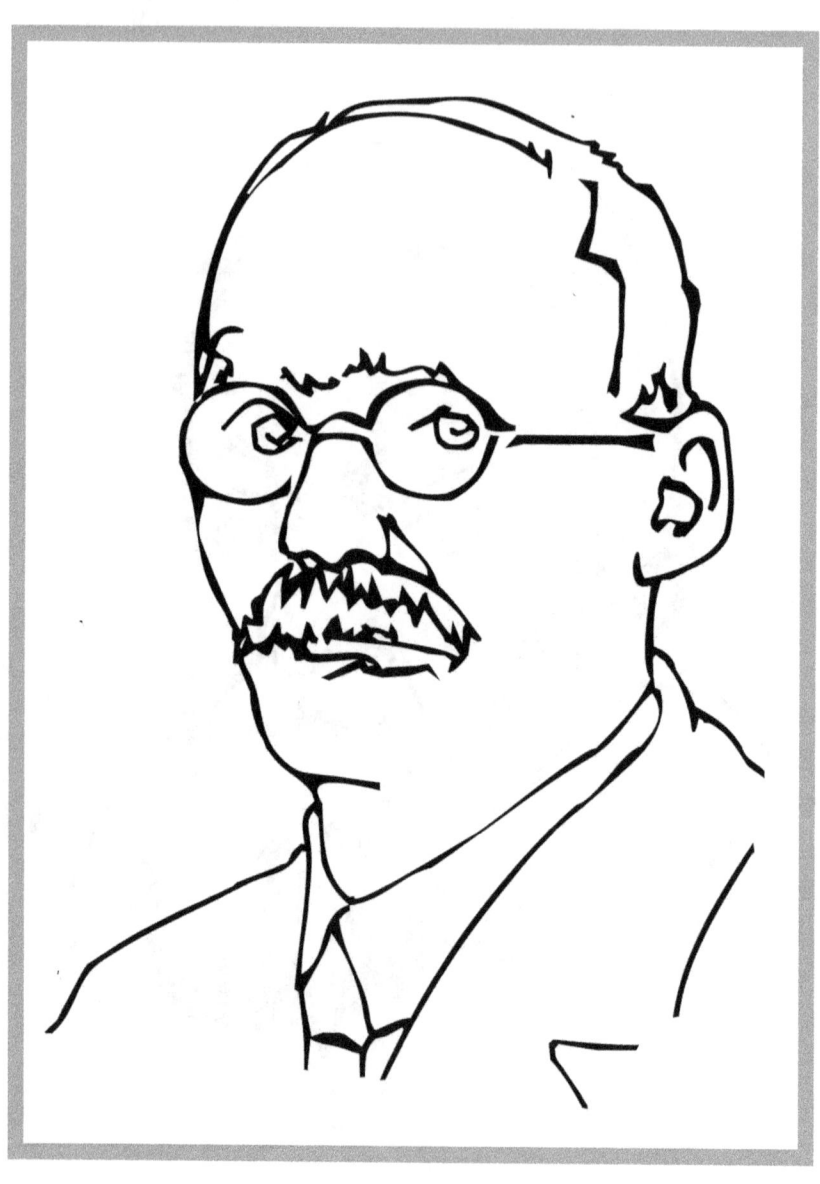

Johannes (Hans) Wilhelm Geiger (1882-1945)

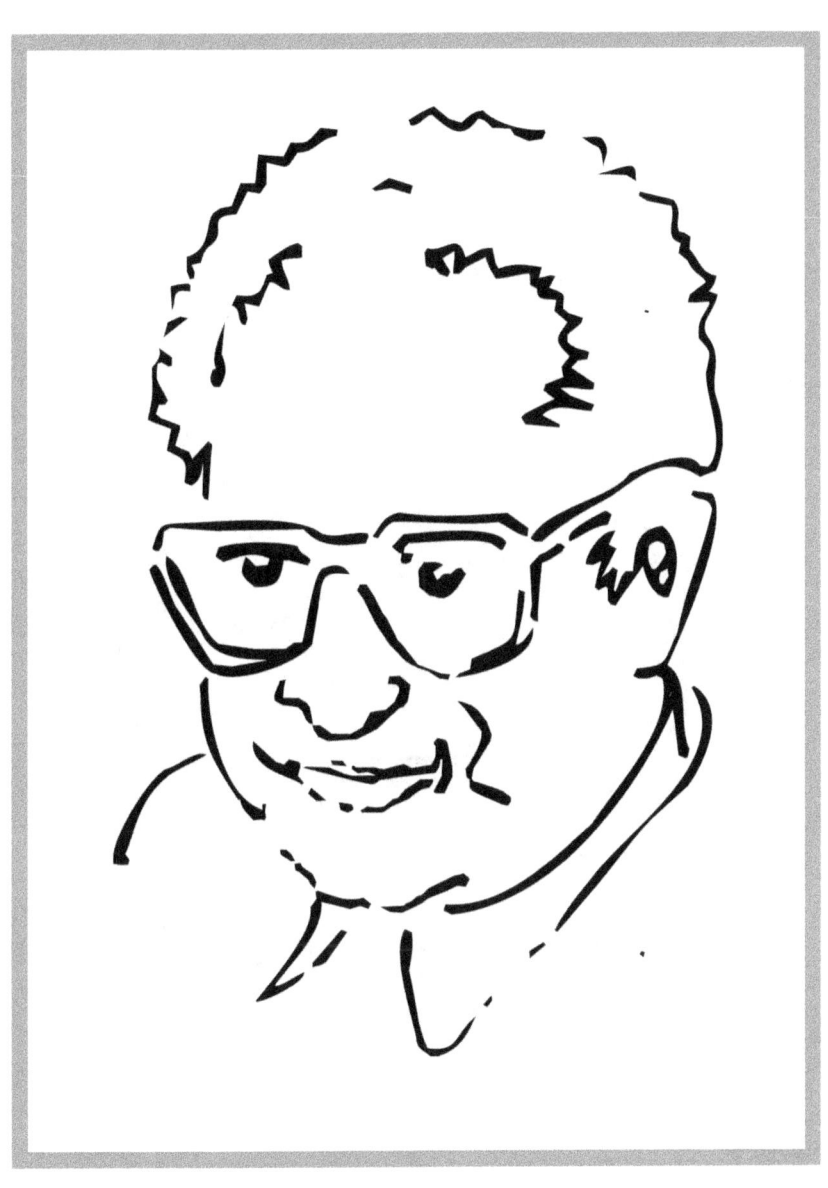

Murray Gell-Mann (1929...)

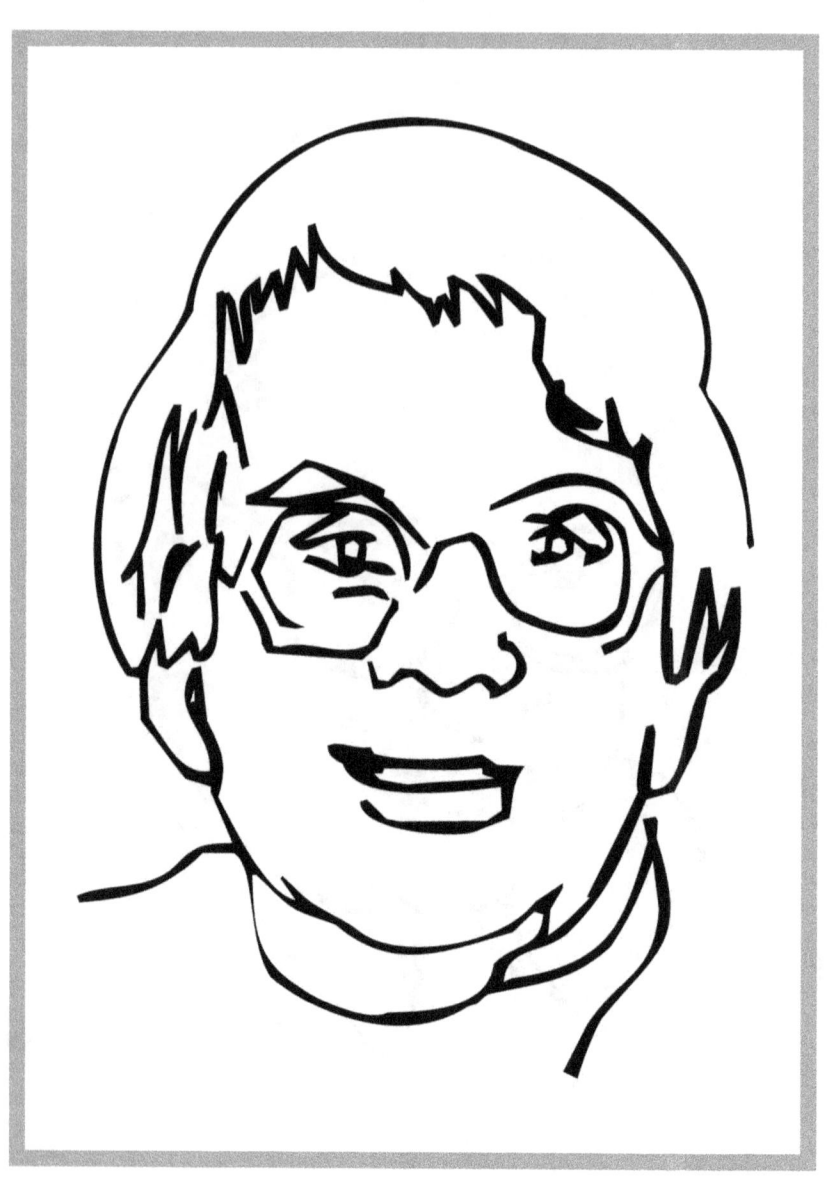

Sheldon Lee Glashow (1932...)

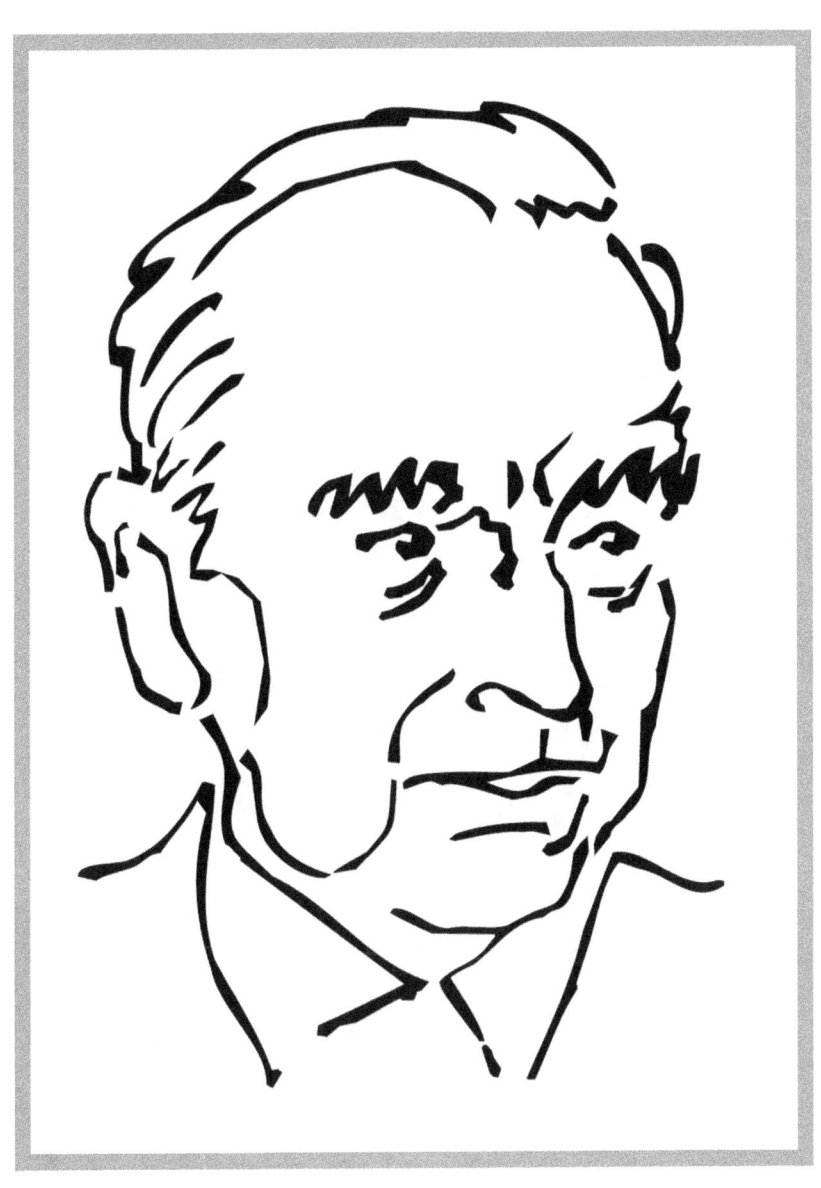

Otto Hahn (1879-1968)

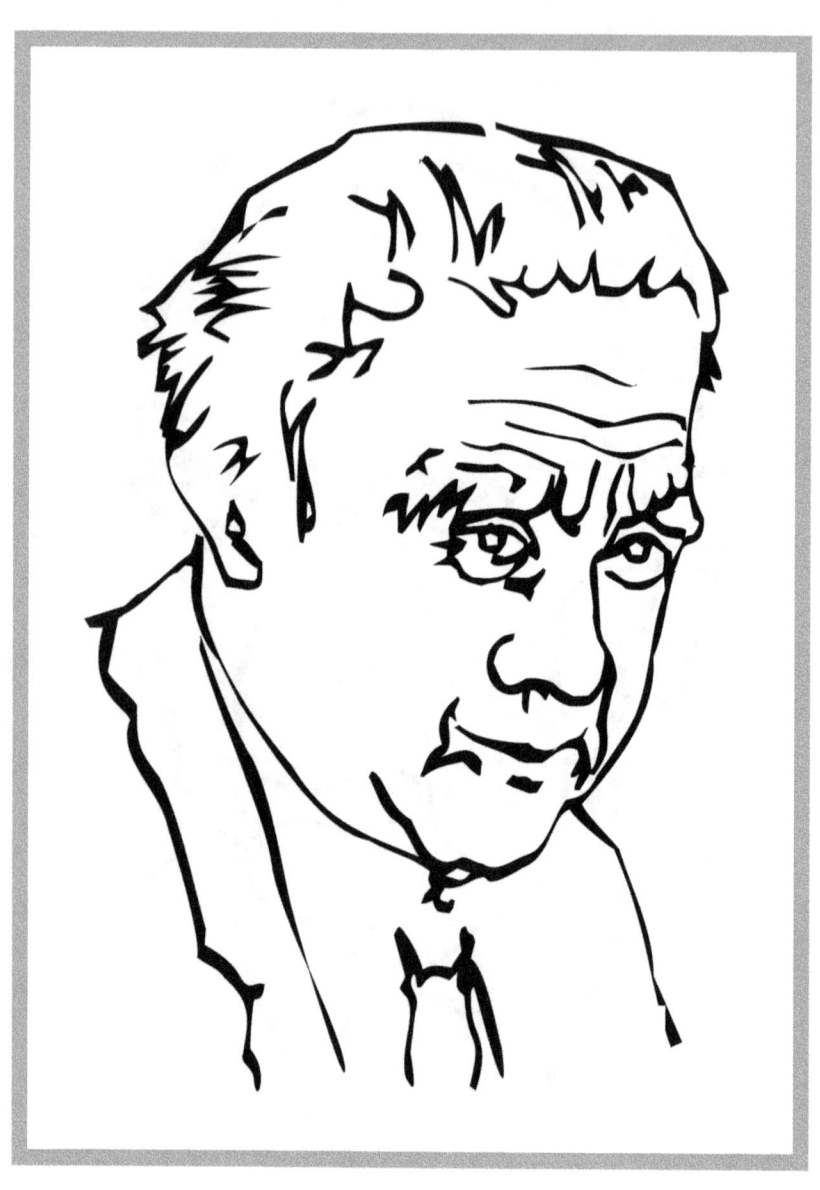

Werner Heisenberg (1901-1976)

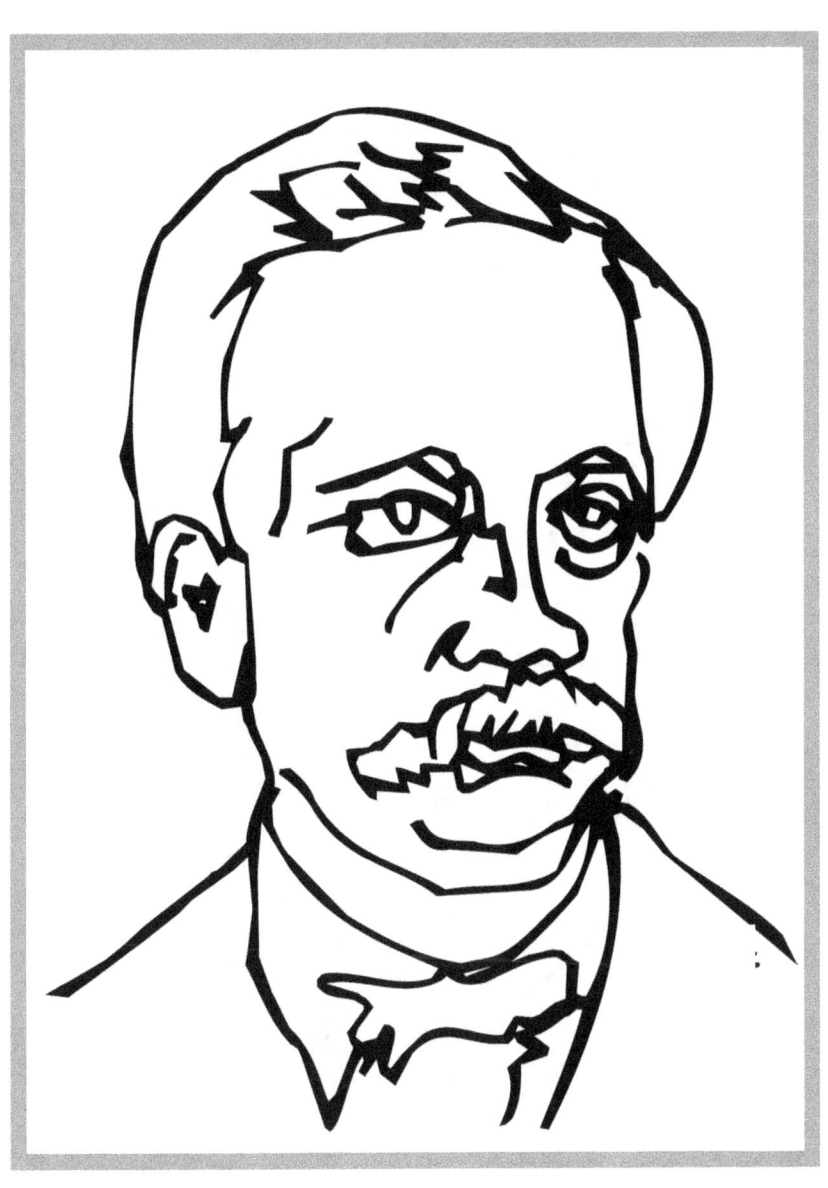

Hermann Ludwig Ferdinand von Helmholtz
(1821-1894)

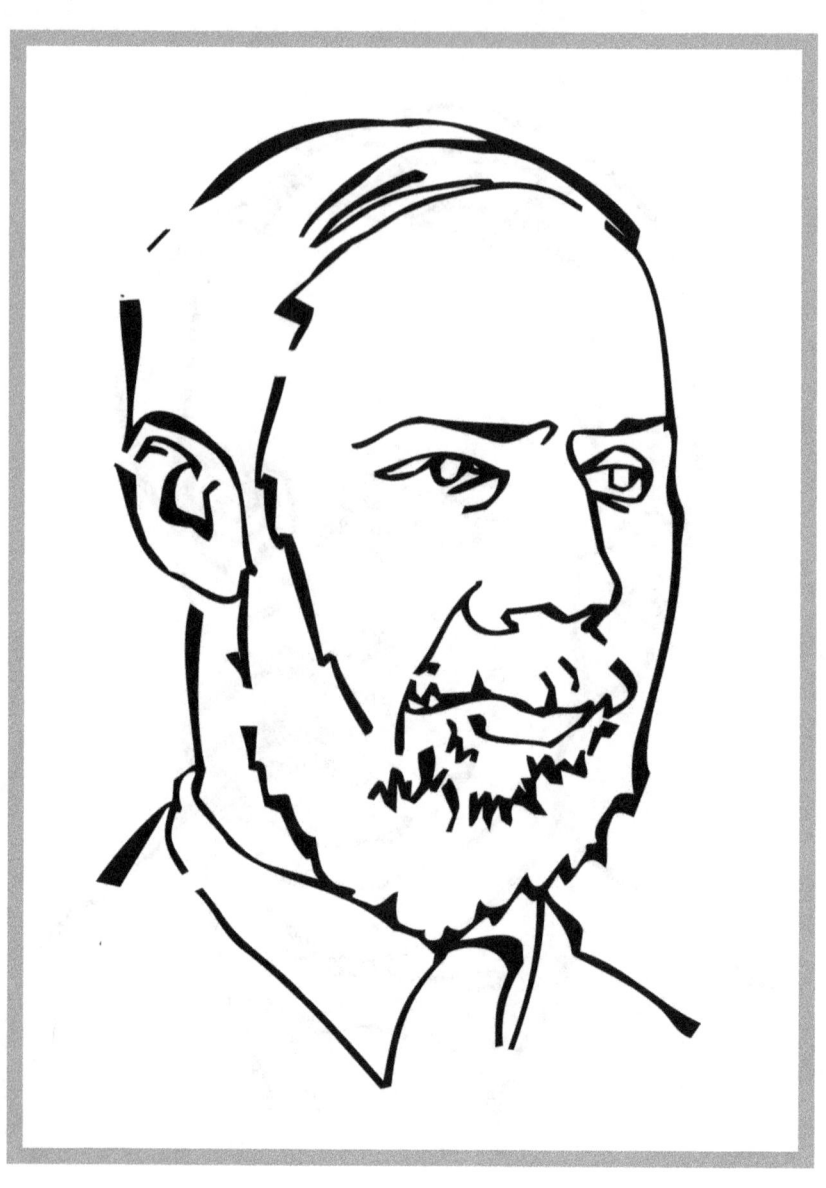

Heinrich Rudolf Hertz (1857-1894)

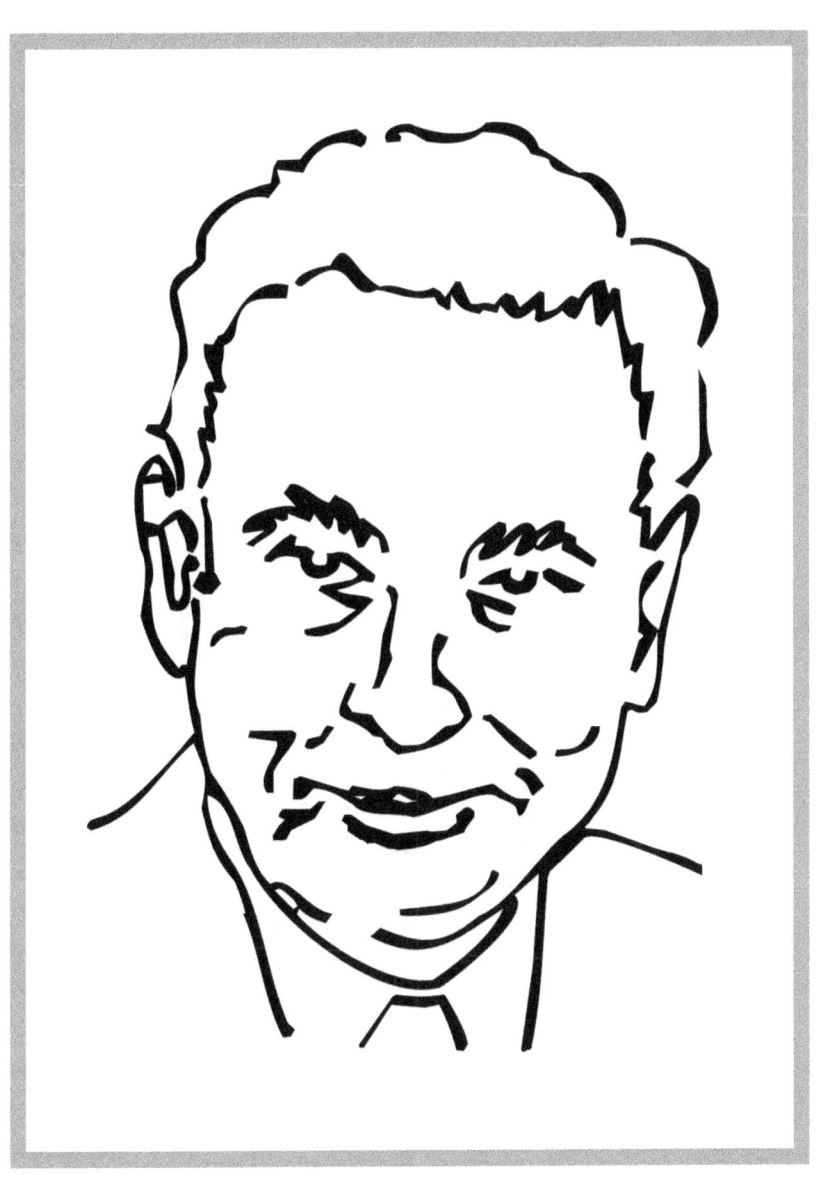

Robert Hofstadter (1915-1990)

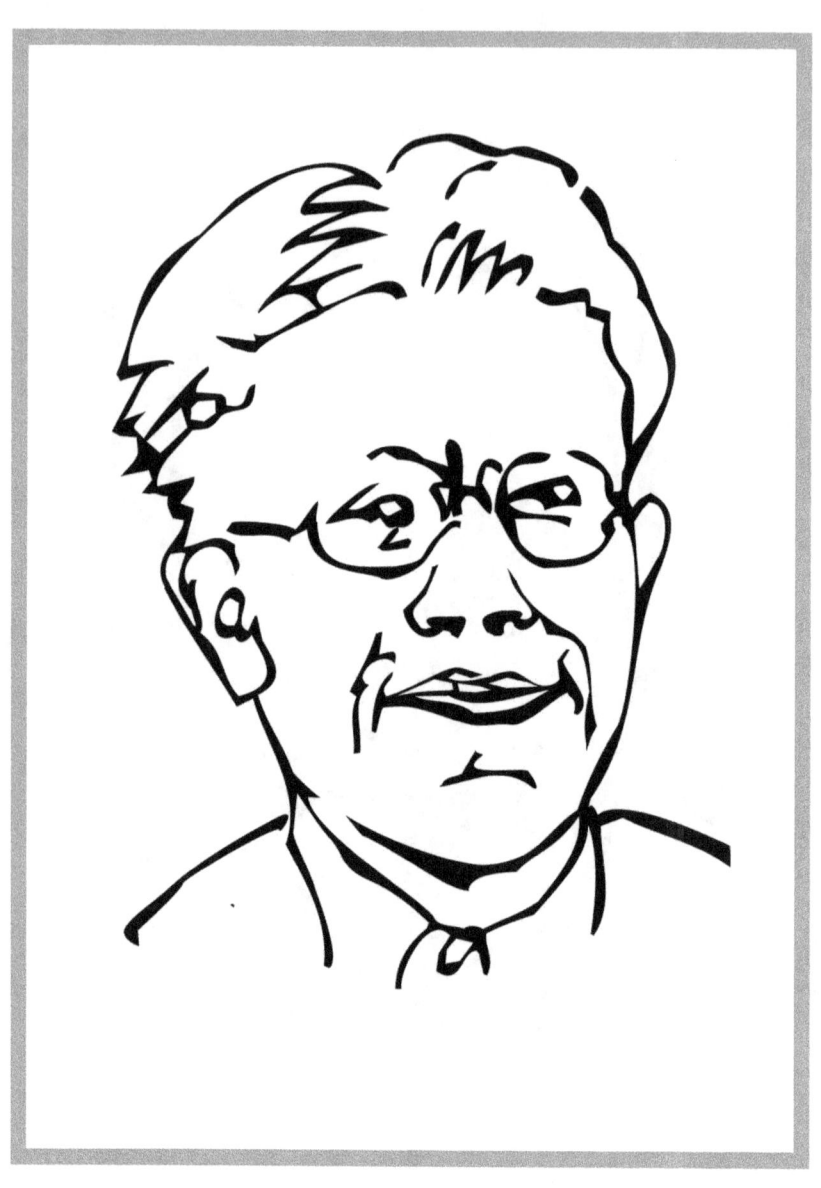

Ernest Orlando Lawrence (1901-1958)

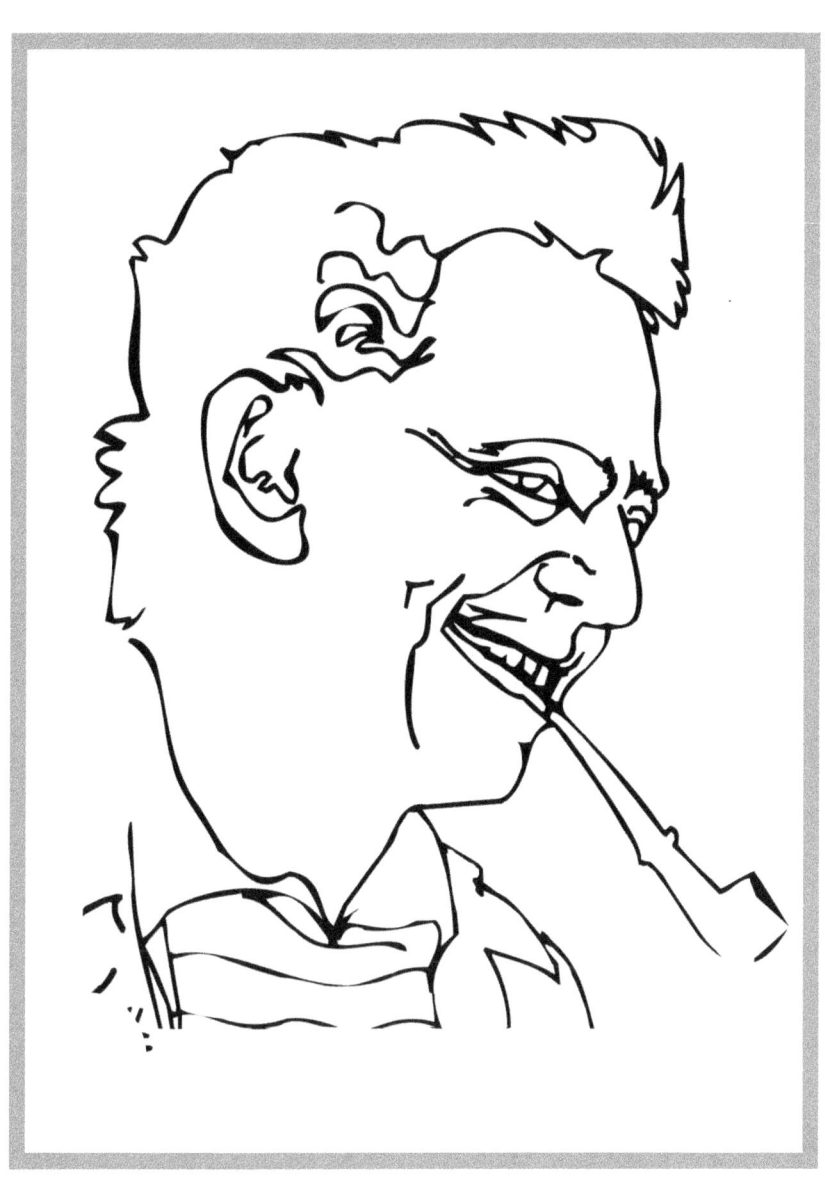

Leon Max Lederman (1922-1990)

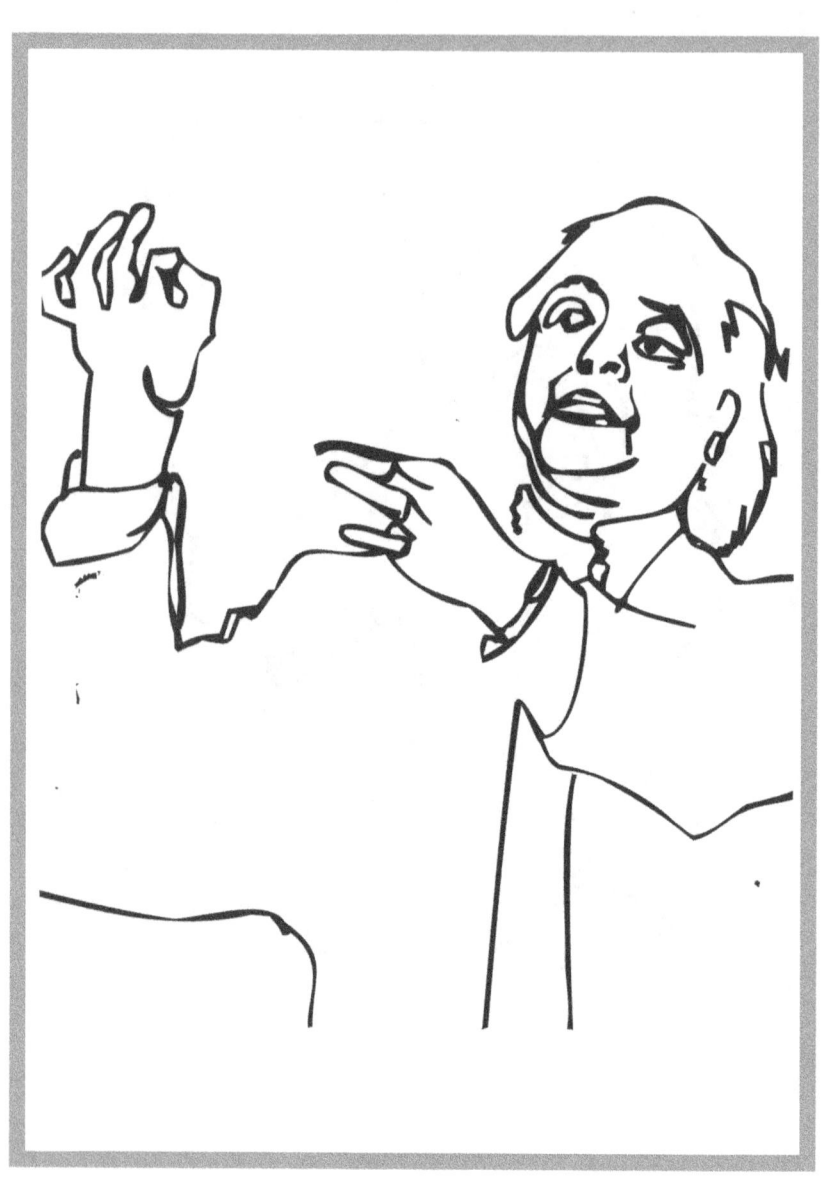

Tsung-Dao Lee (1926...)

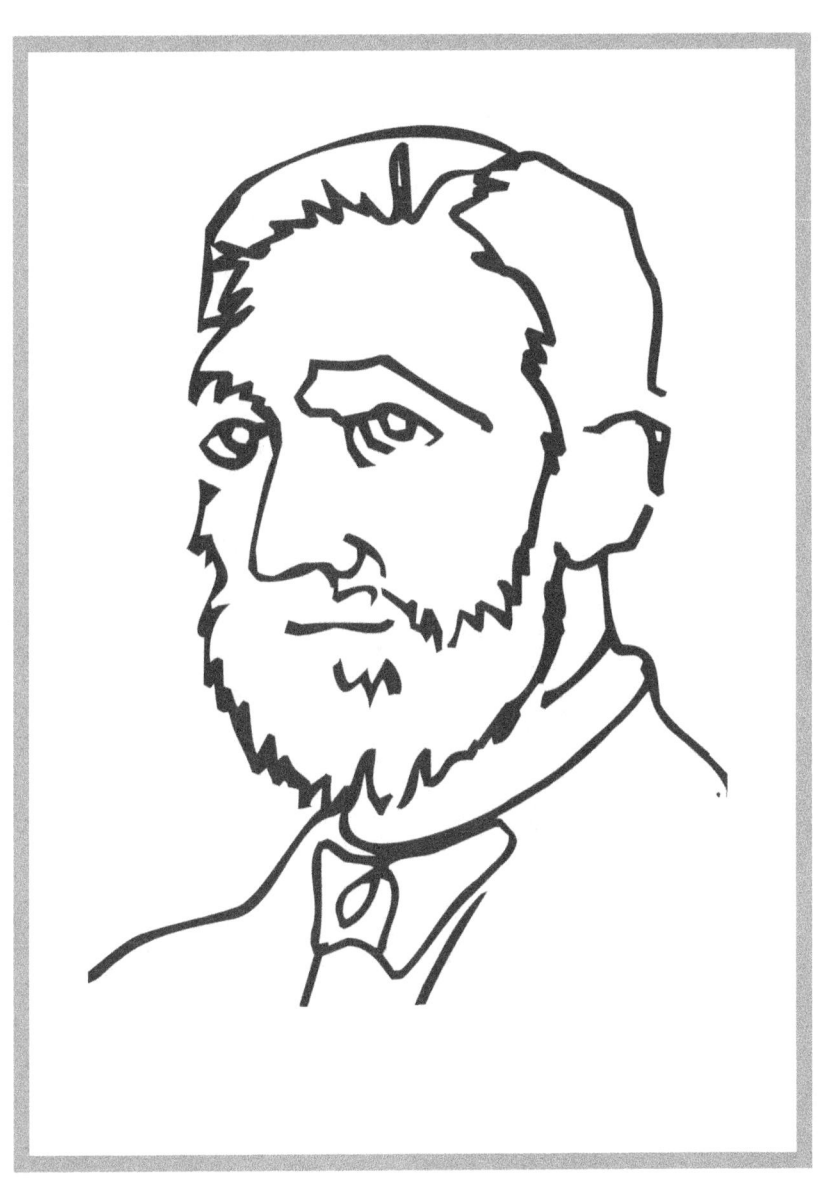

Philipp von Lenard (1862-1947)

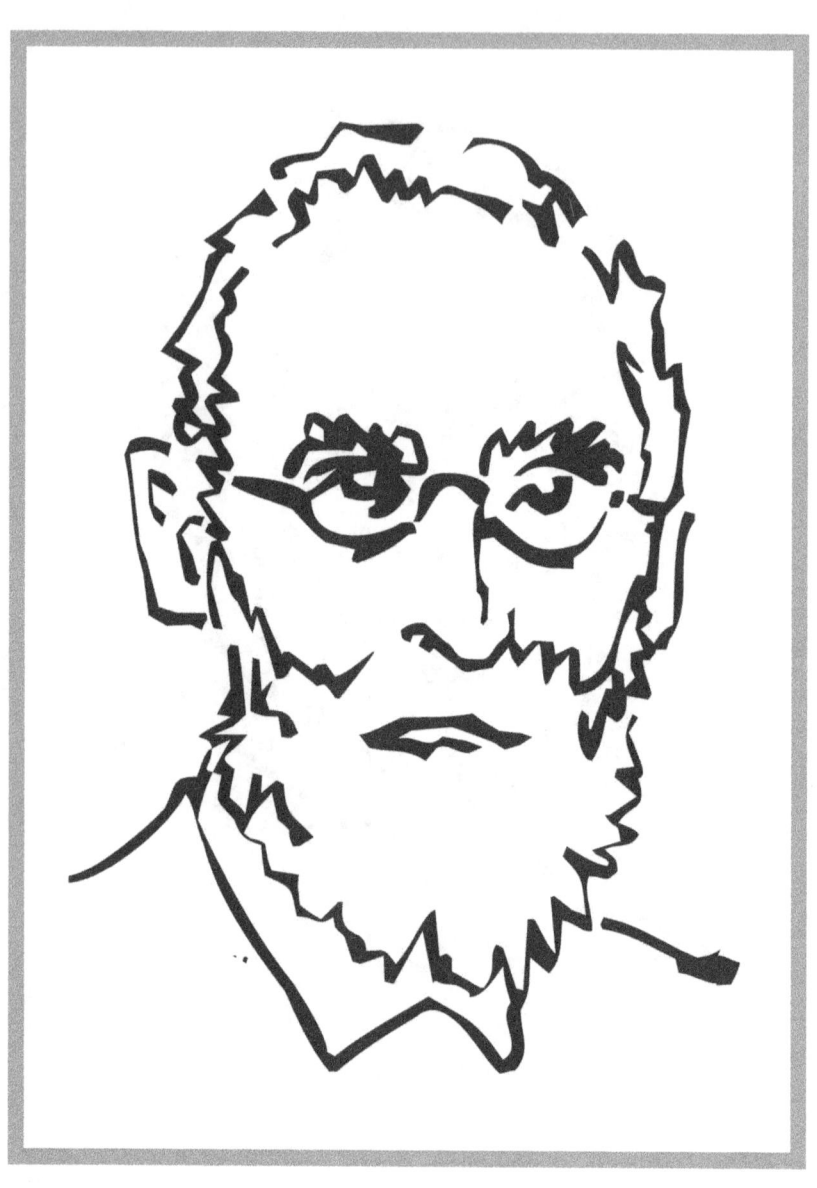

Hendrik Antoon Lorentz (1853-1928)

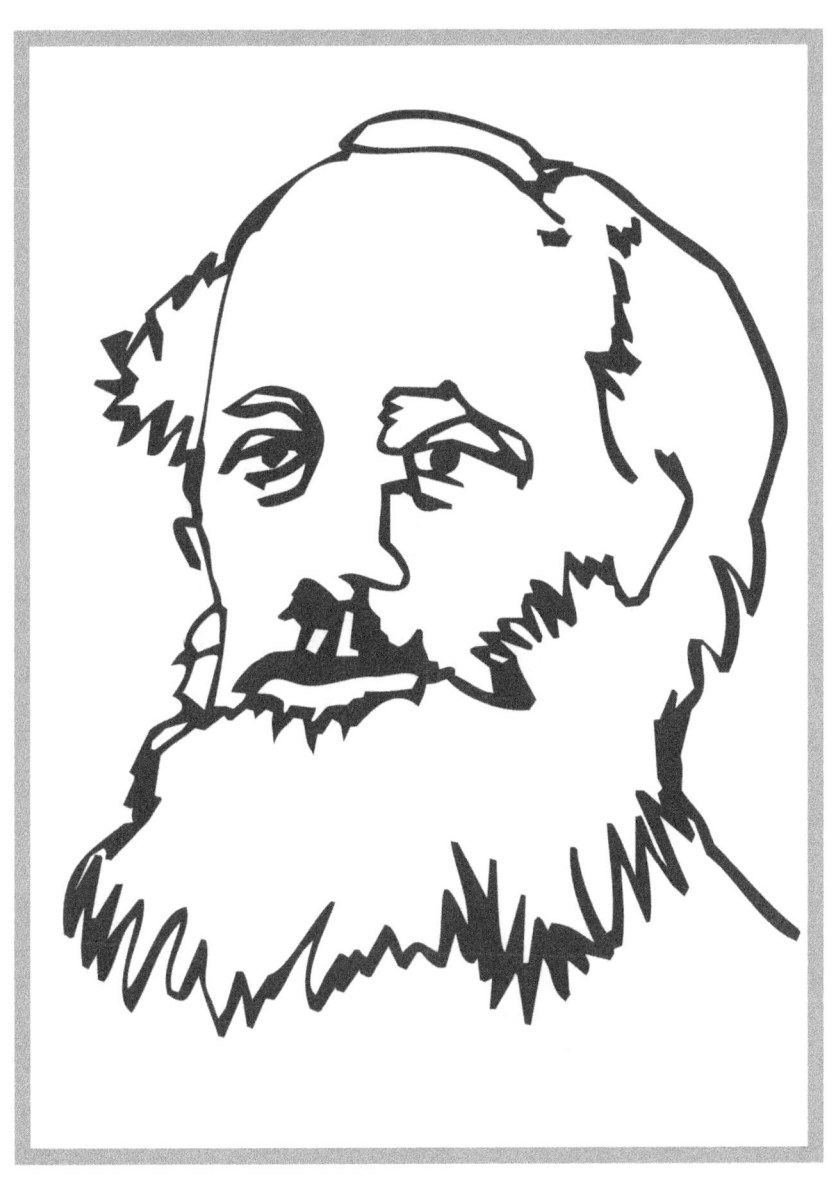

James Clerk Maxwell (1831-1879)

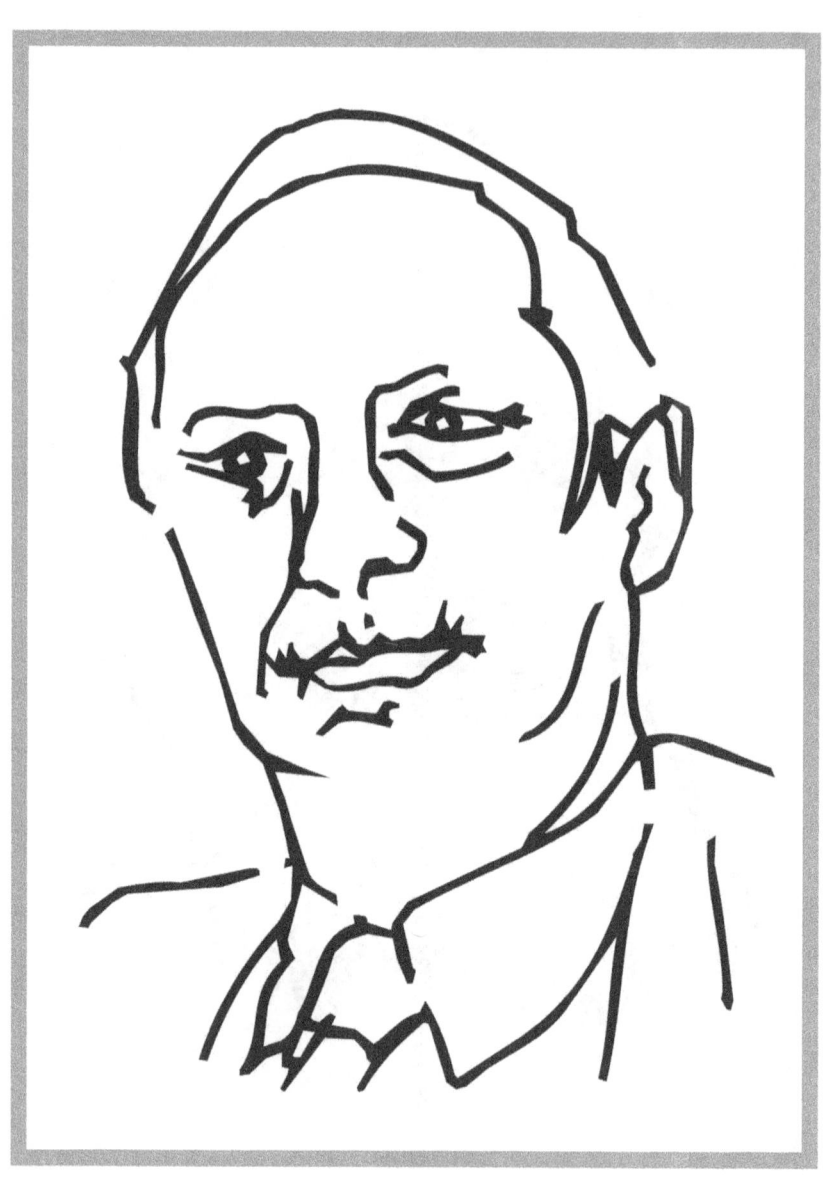

Simon van der Meer (1925...)

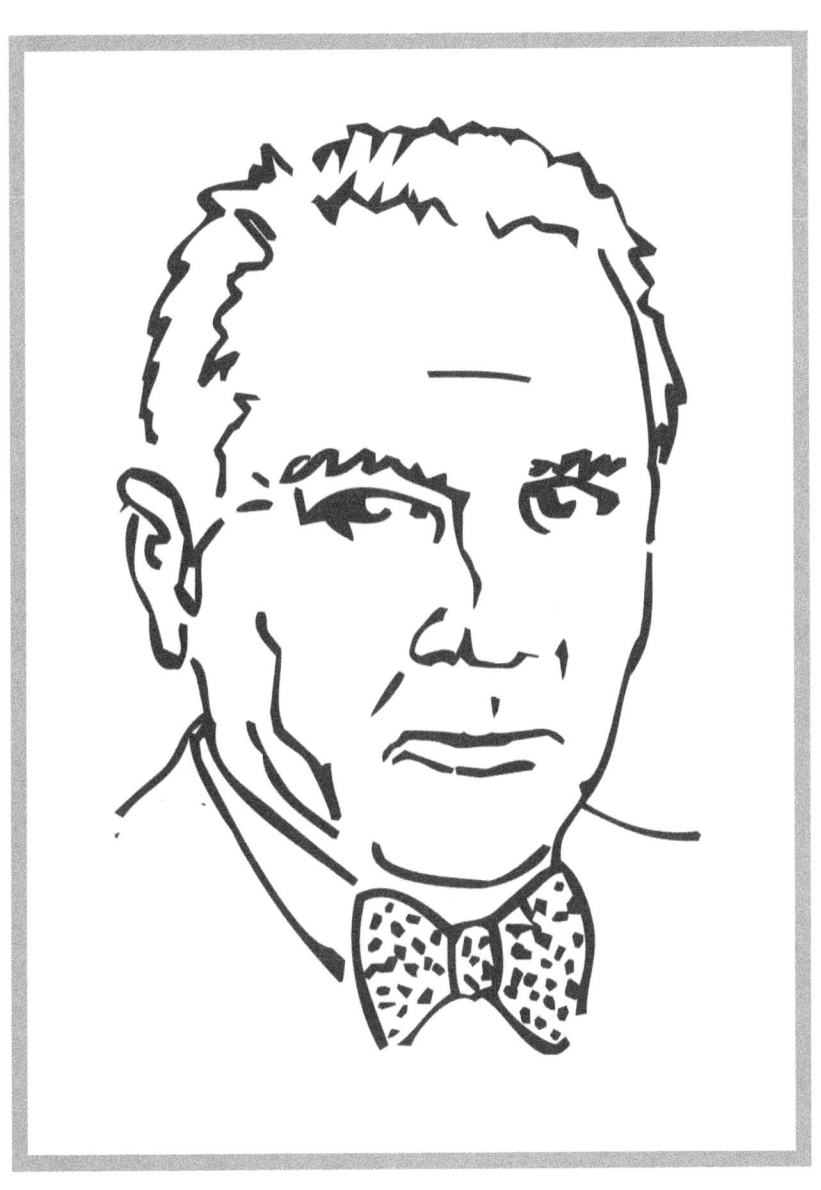

Robert Andrews Millikan (1868-1953)

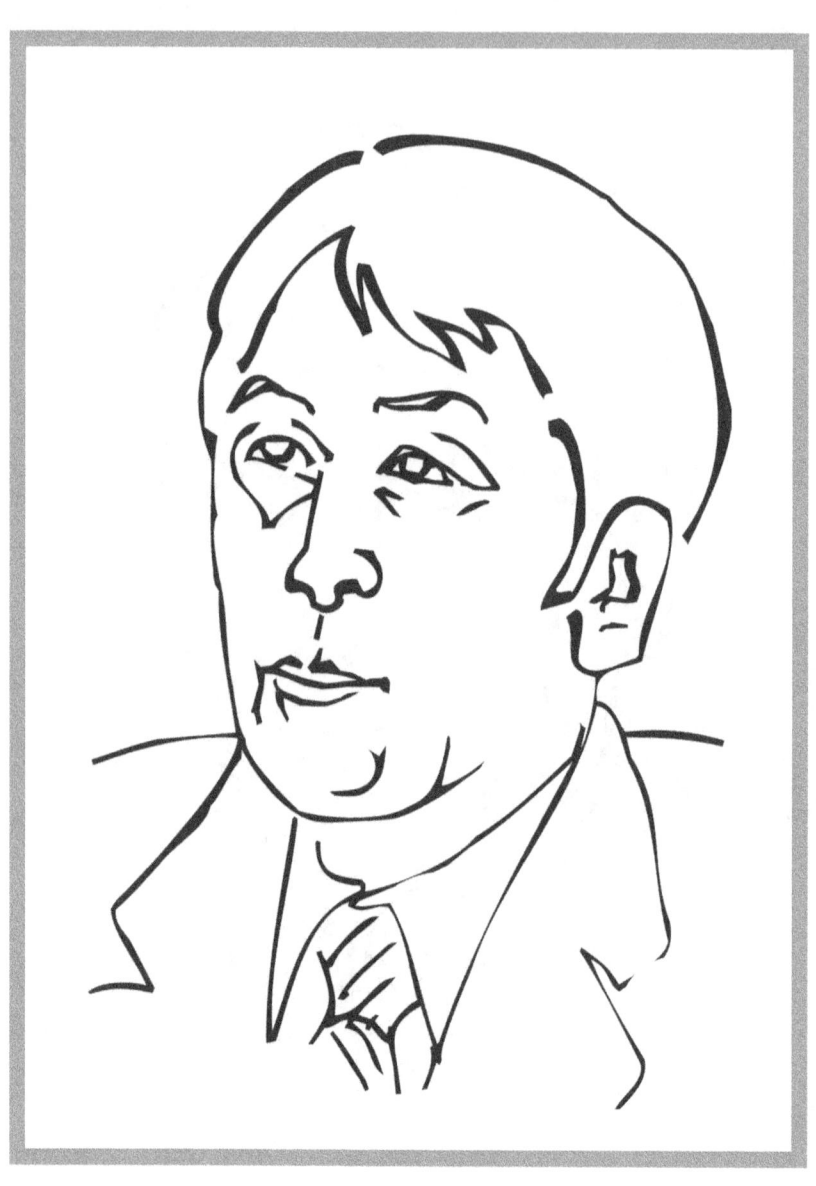

Yoichiro Nambu (1921...)

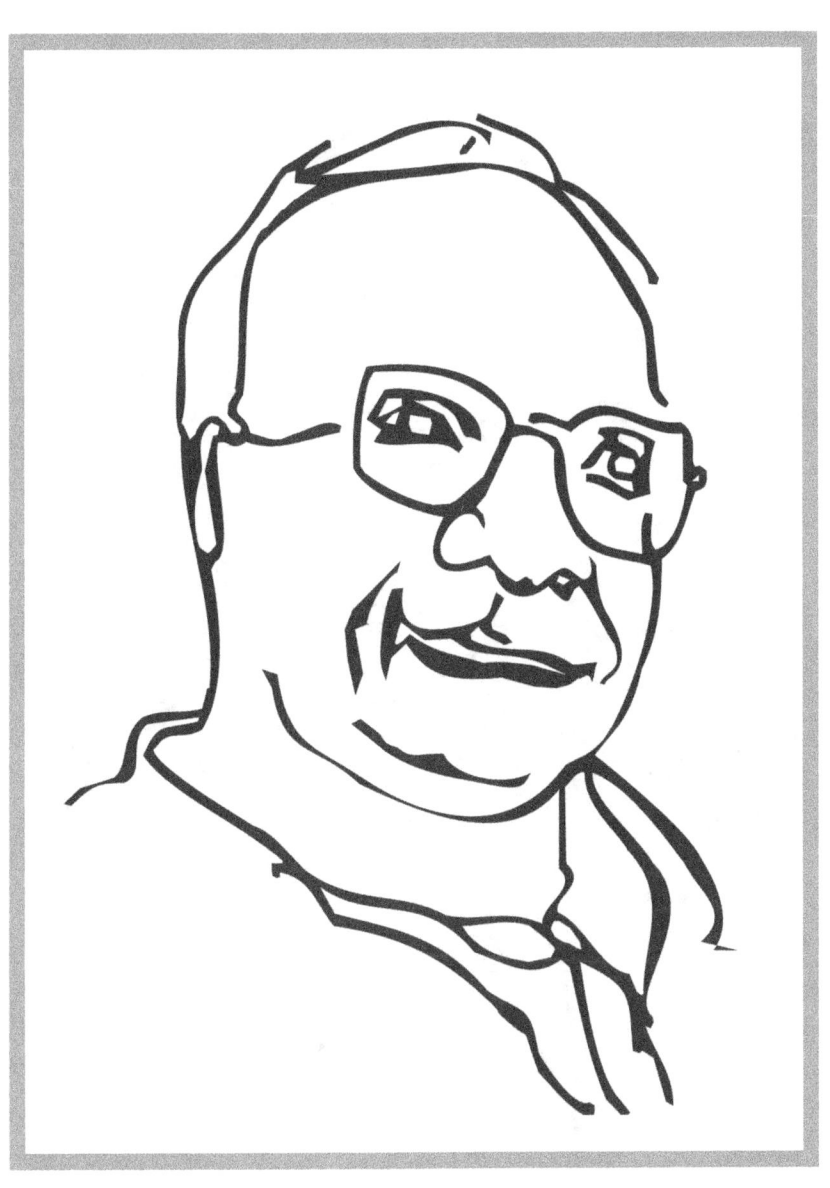

Yuval Ne'eman (1925...)

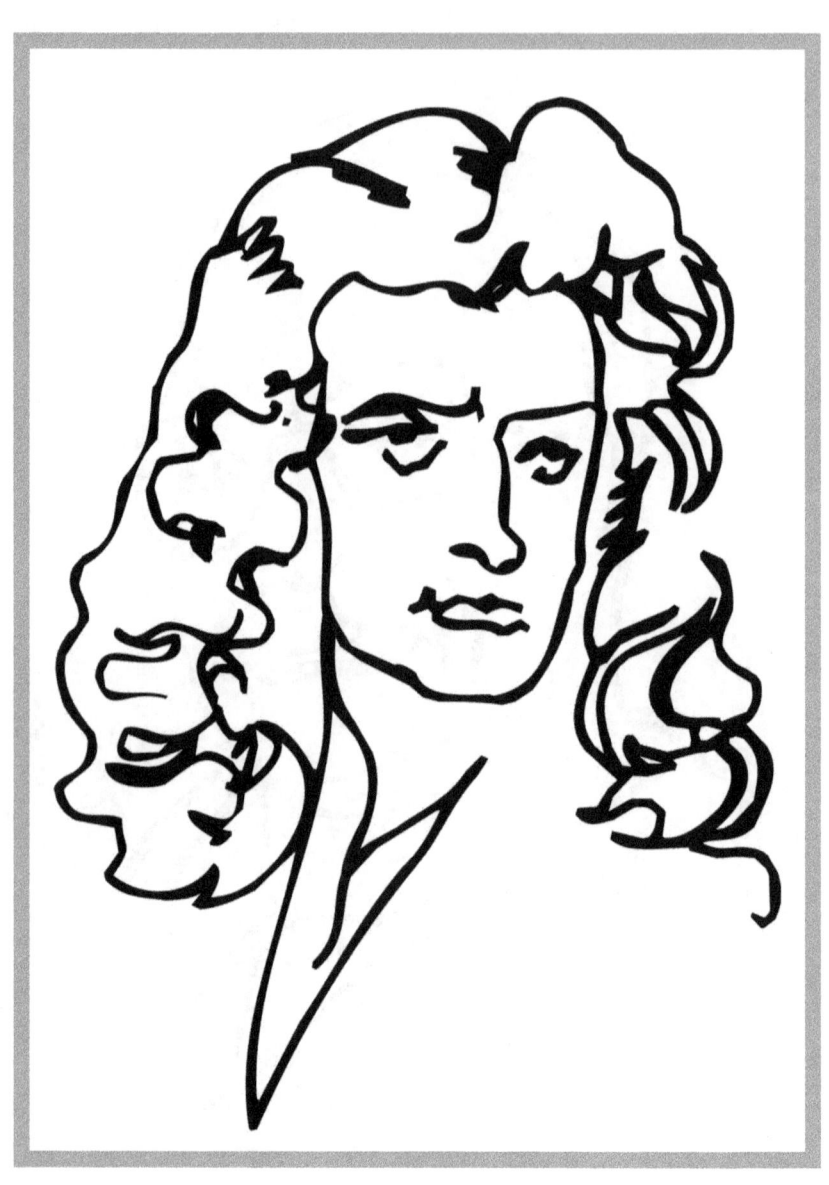

Isaac Newton (1643-1727)

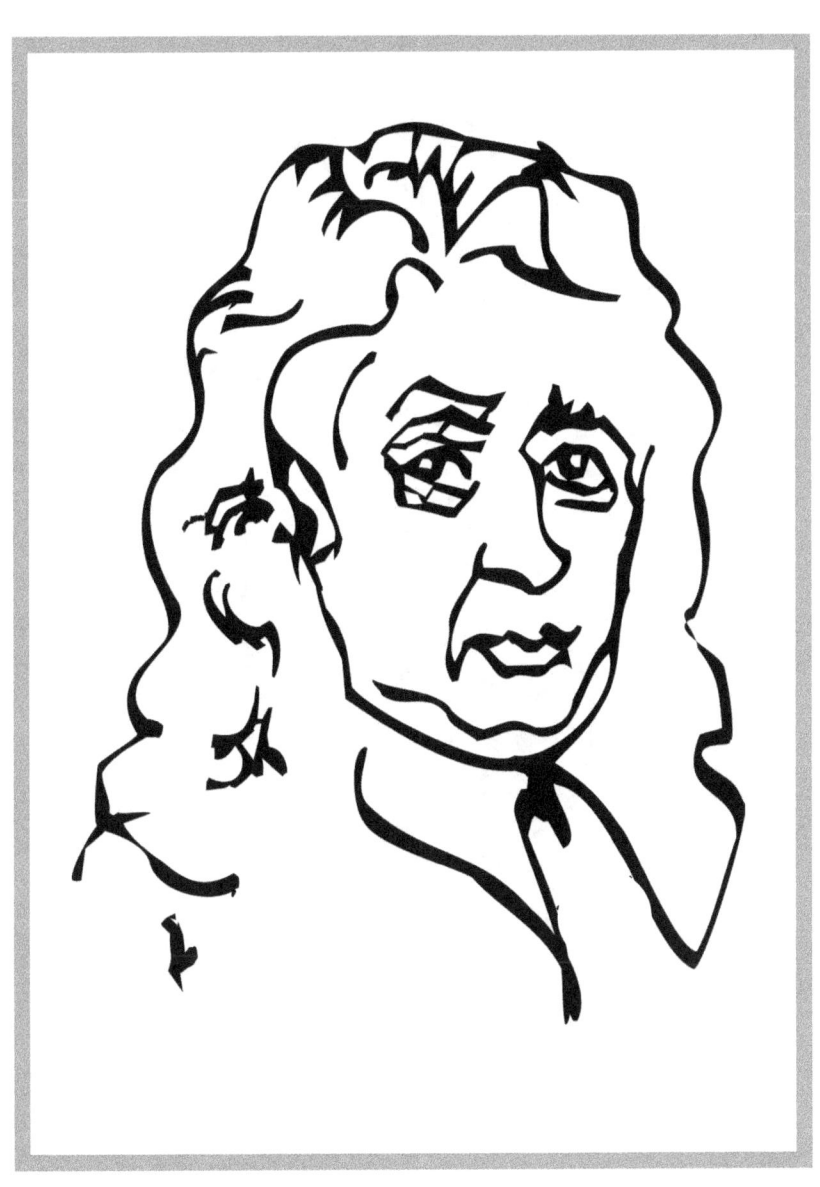

Isaac Newton (1643-1727)

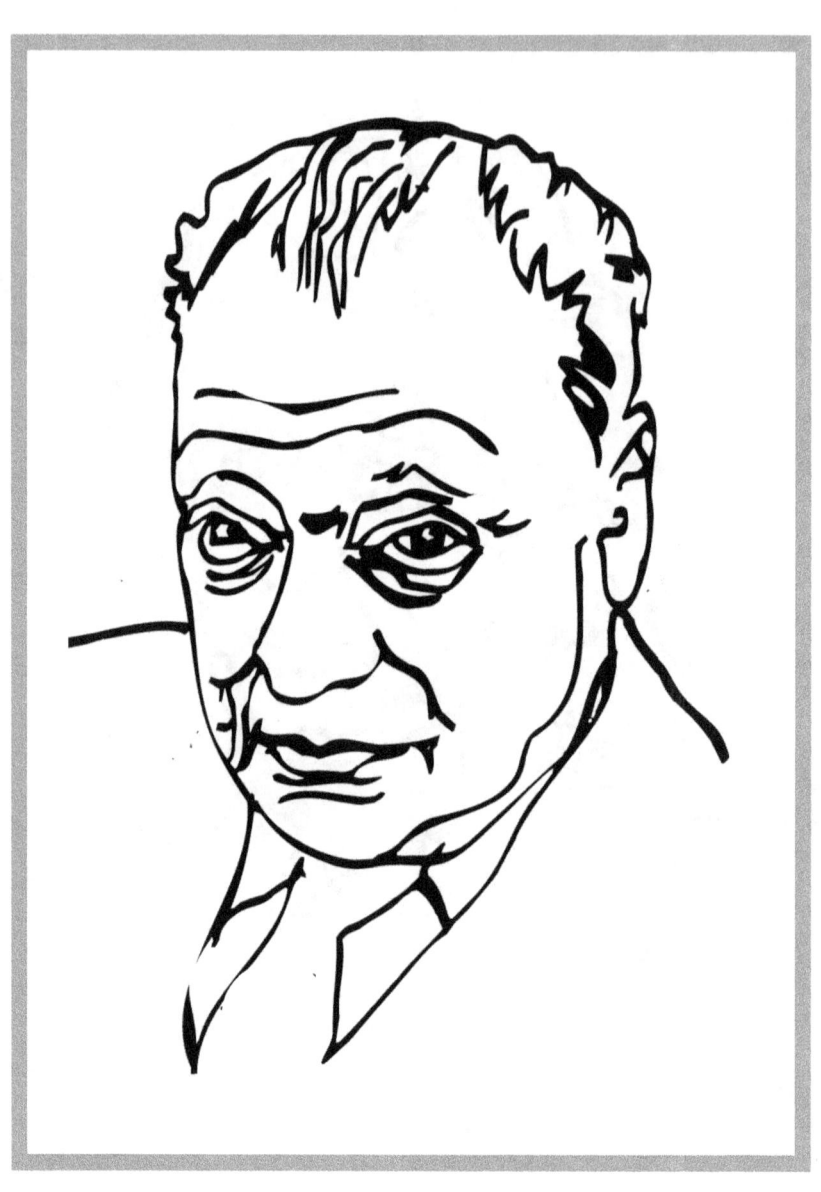

Wolfgang Pauli (1900-1958)

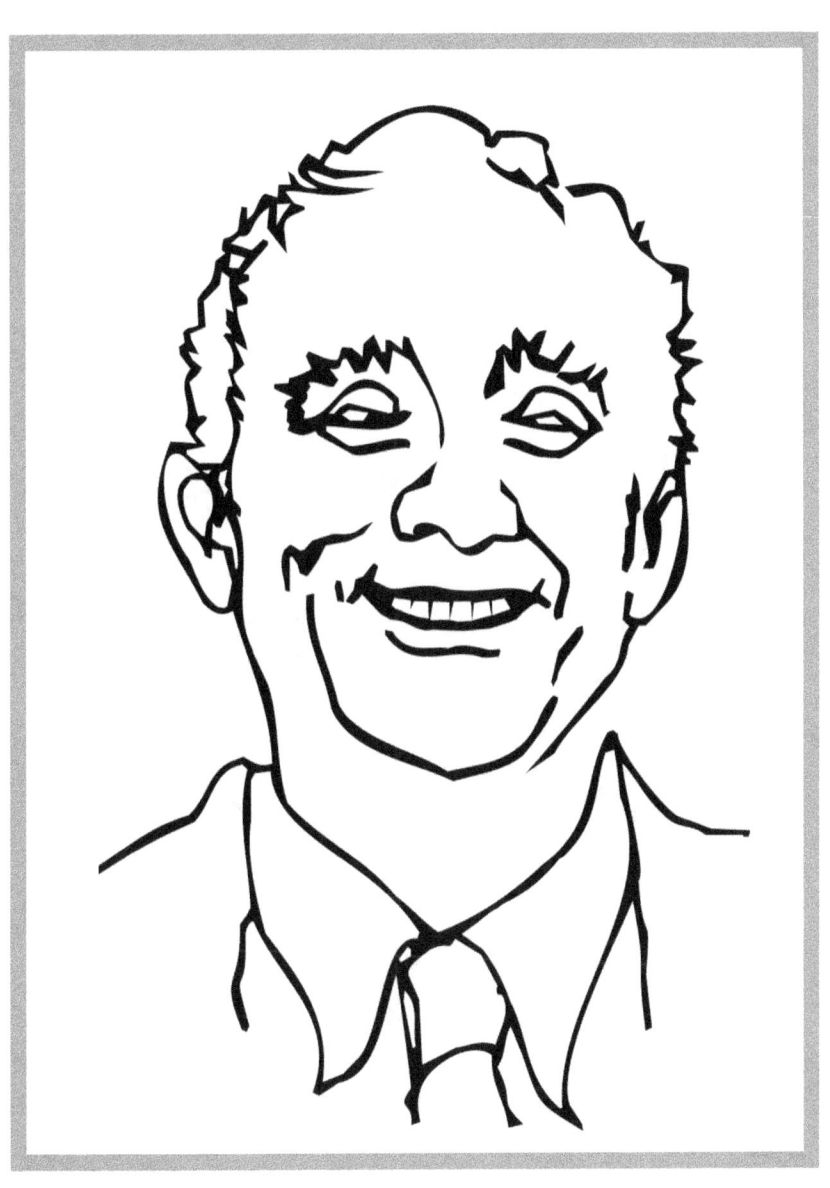

Martin Lewis Perl (1920...)

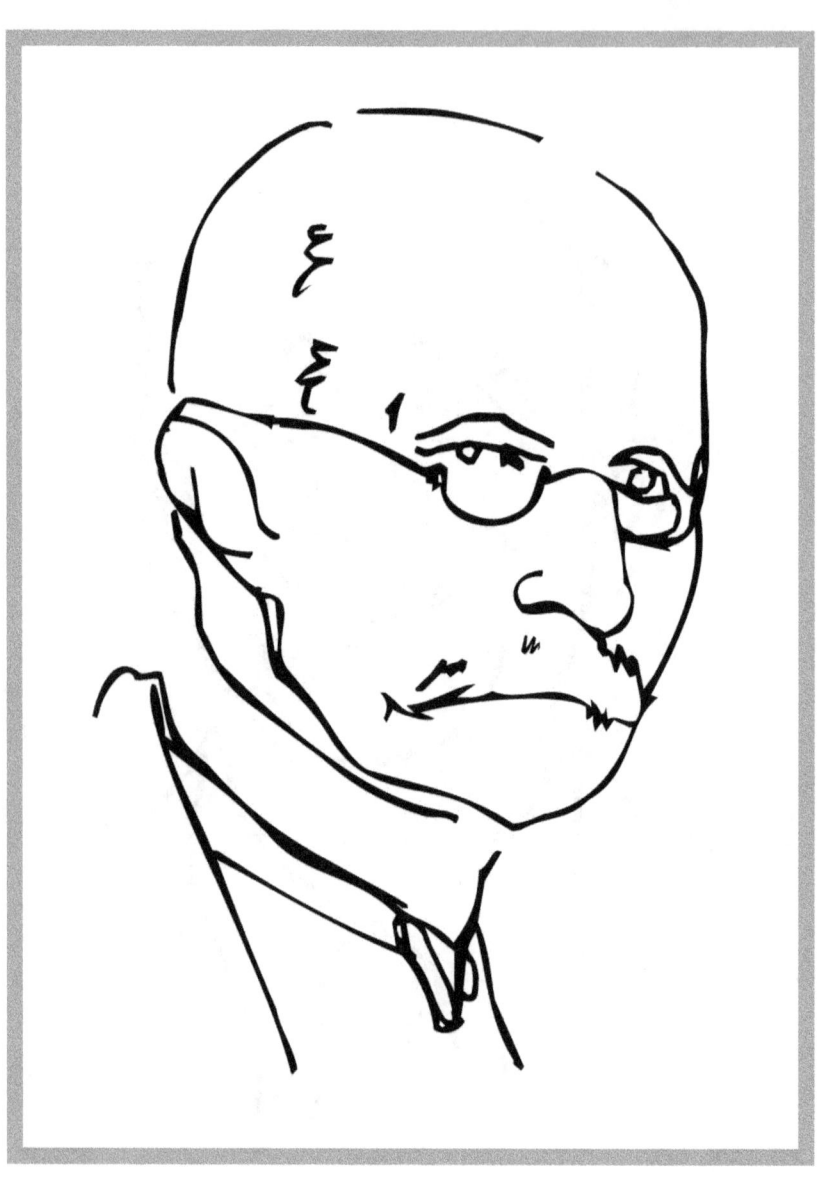

Max Planck (1858-1947)

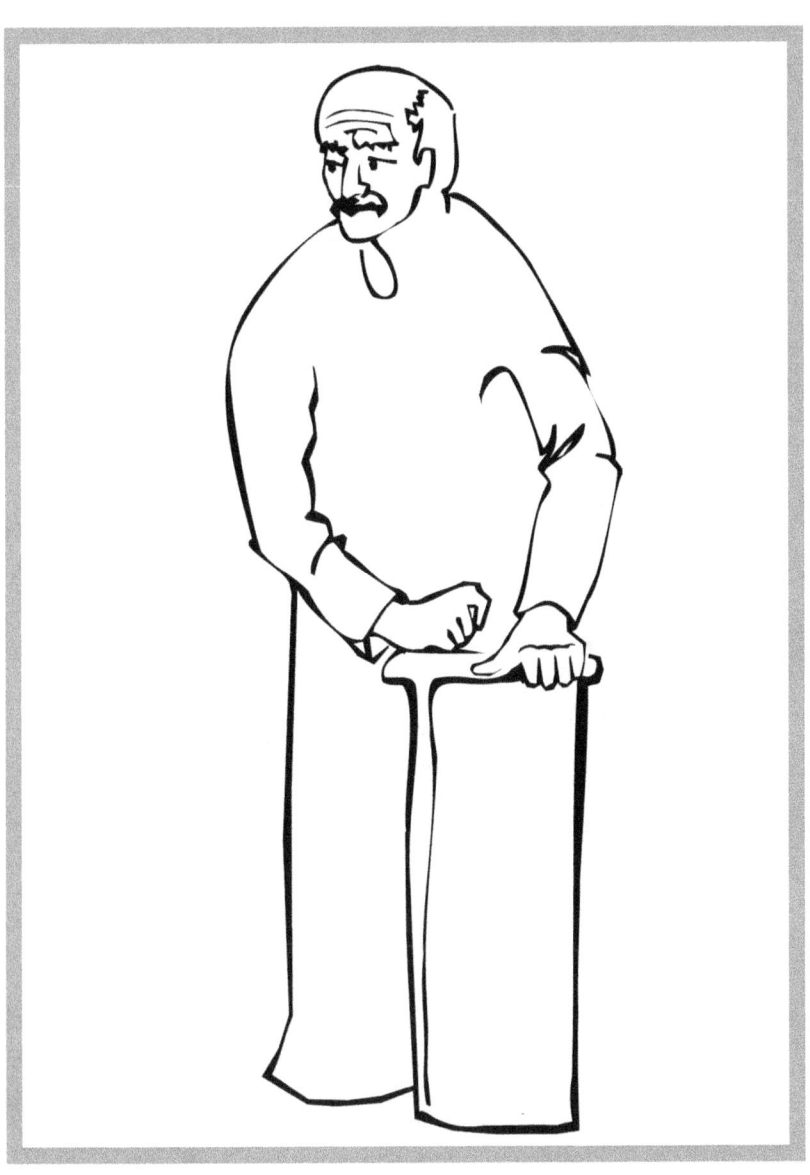

Max Planck (1858-1947)
Denkmal – *Monumento* – Memorial
DESY-Zeuthen

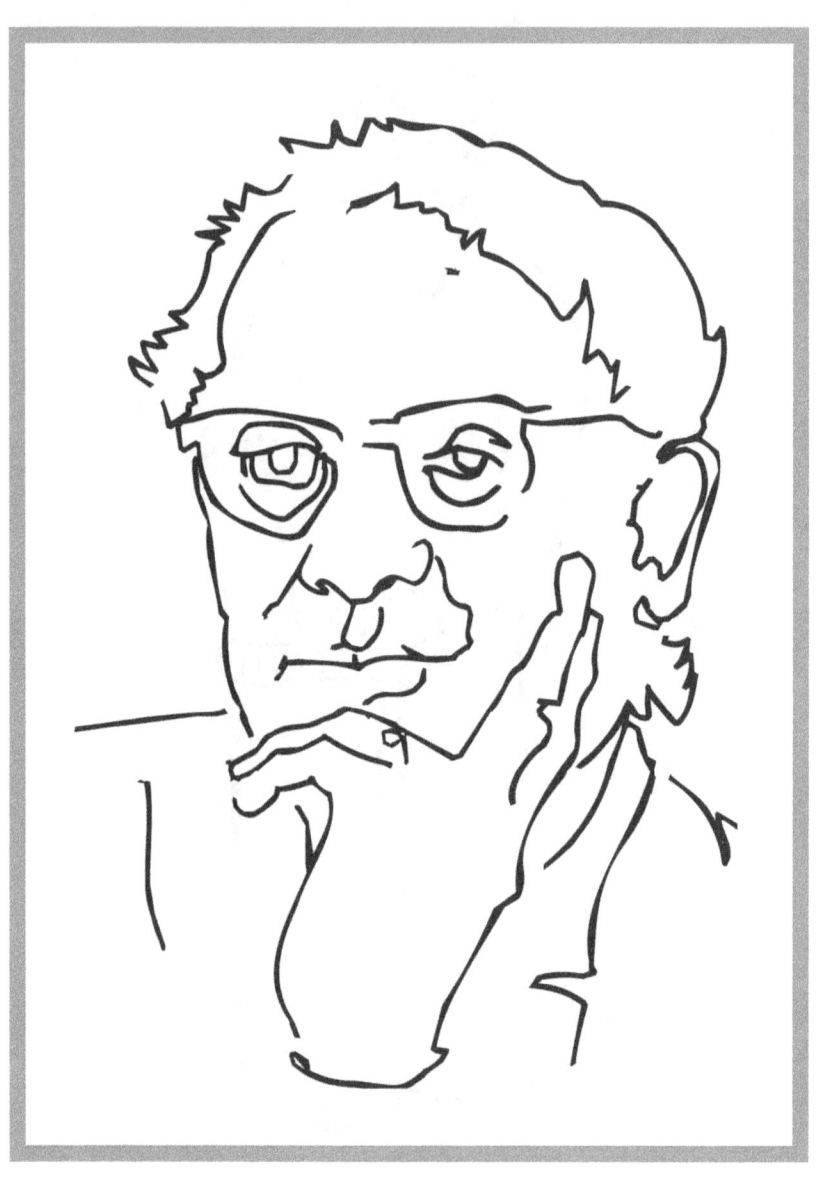

Frederick Reines (1918-1998)

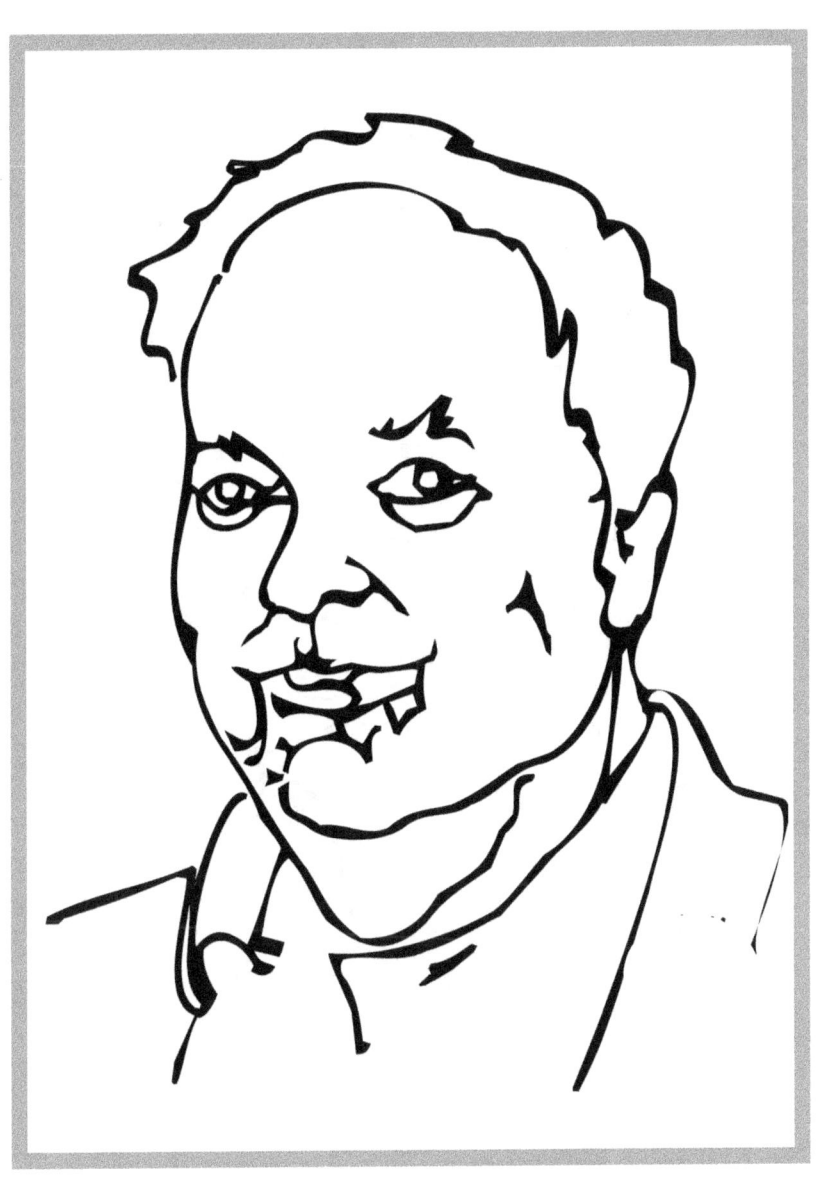

Burton Richter (1931...)

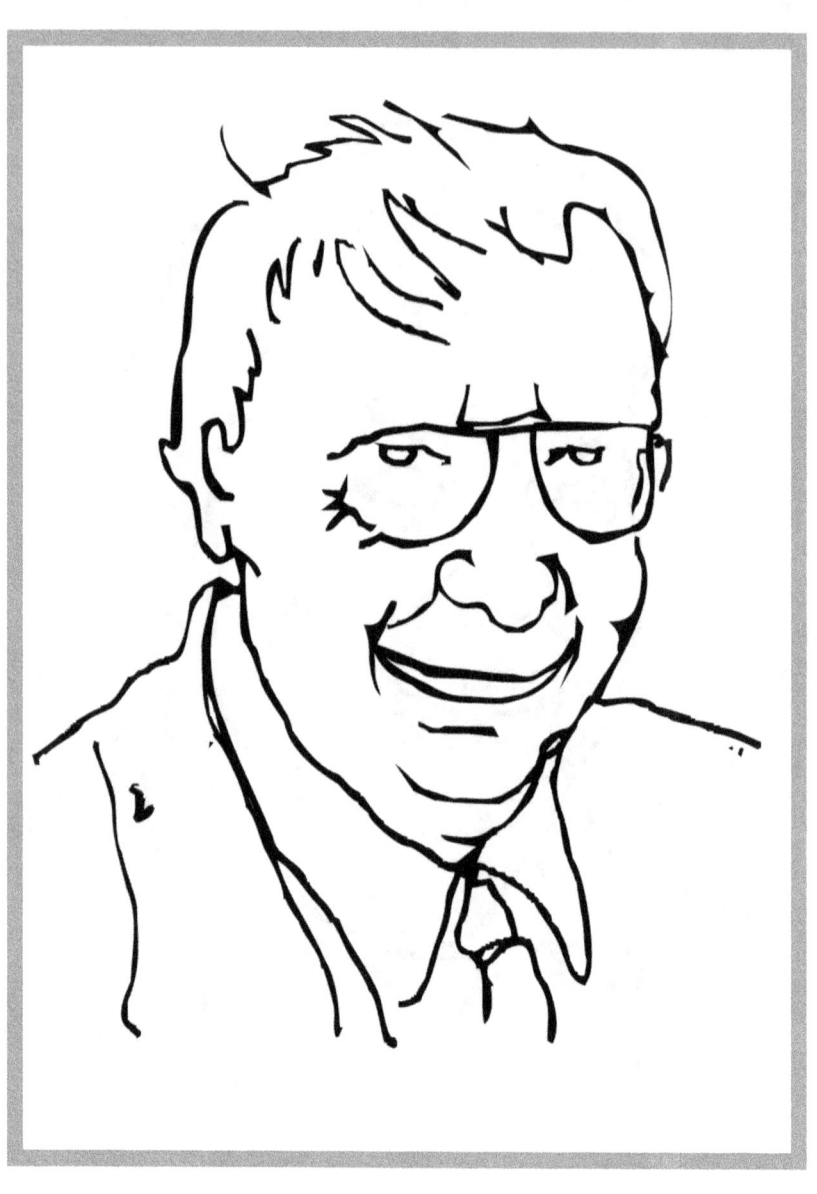

Carlo Rubbia (1934...)

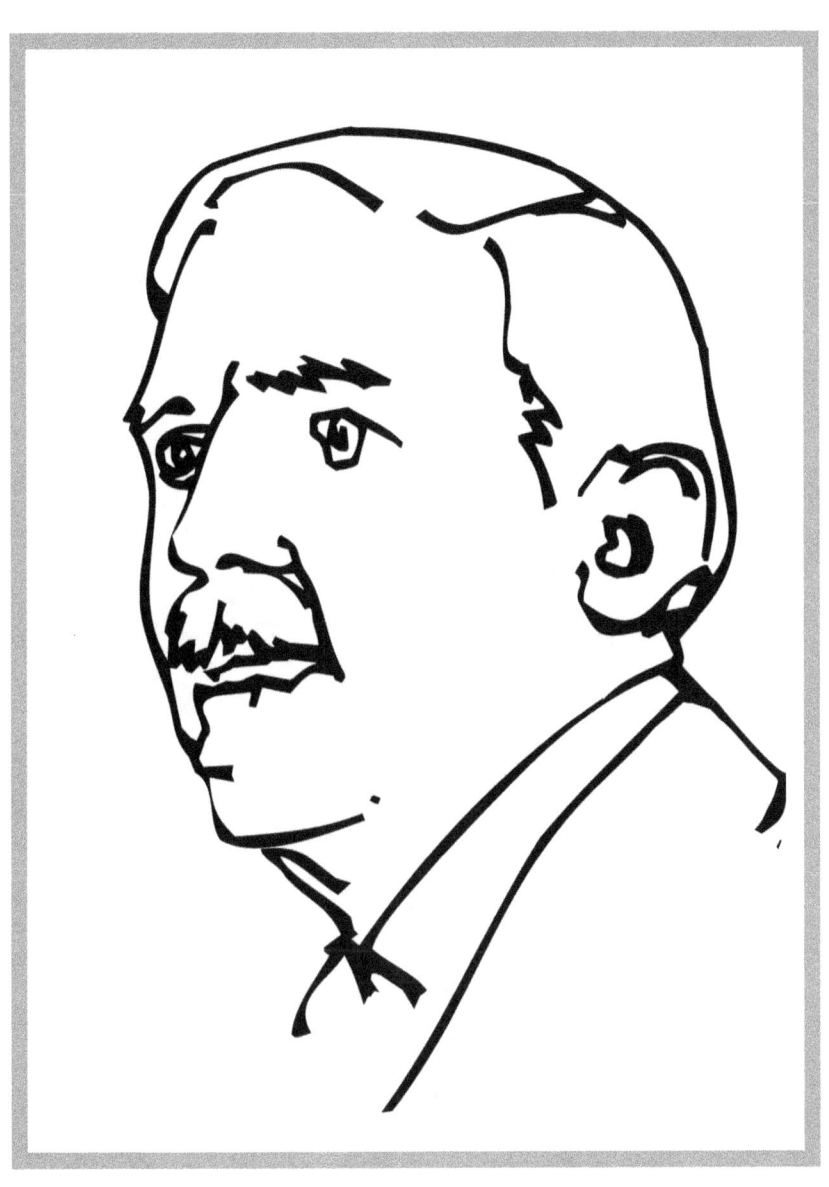

Ernest Rutherford (1871-1937)

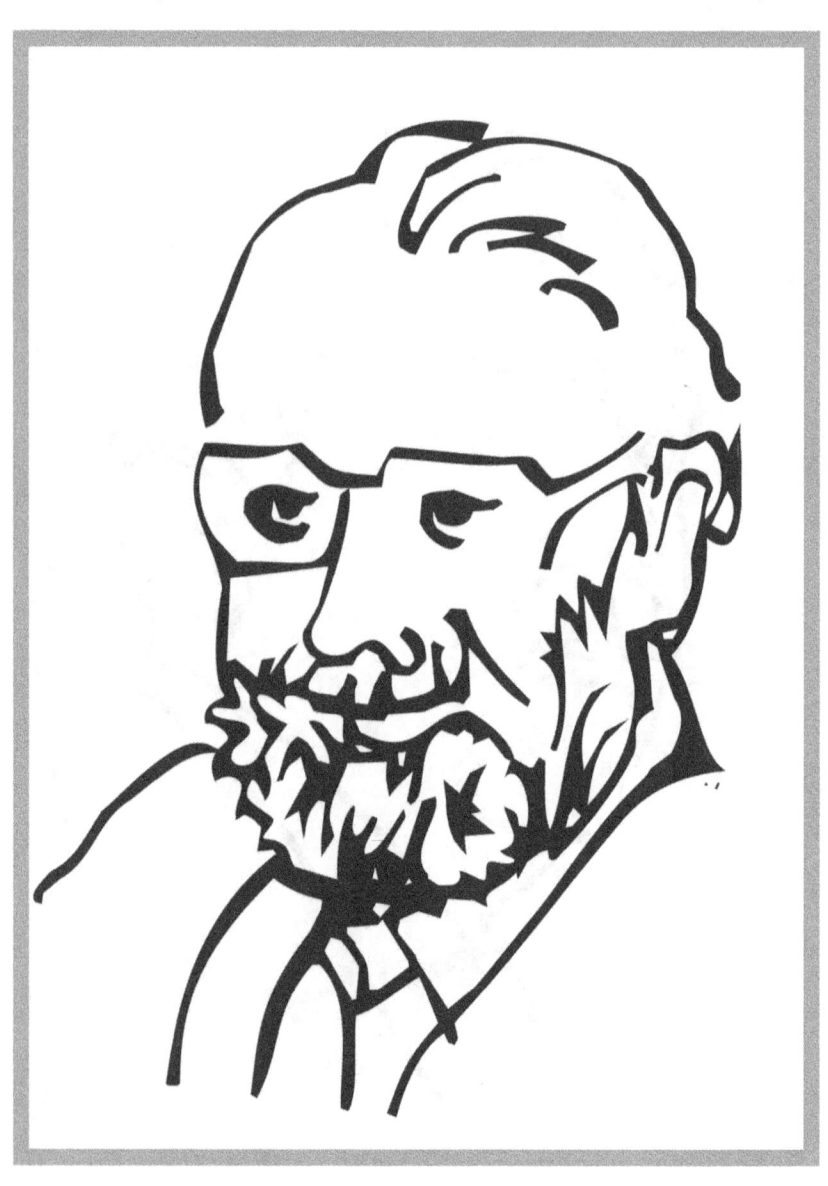

Abdus Salam (1926-1996)

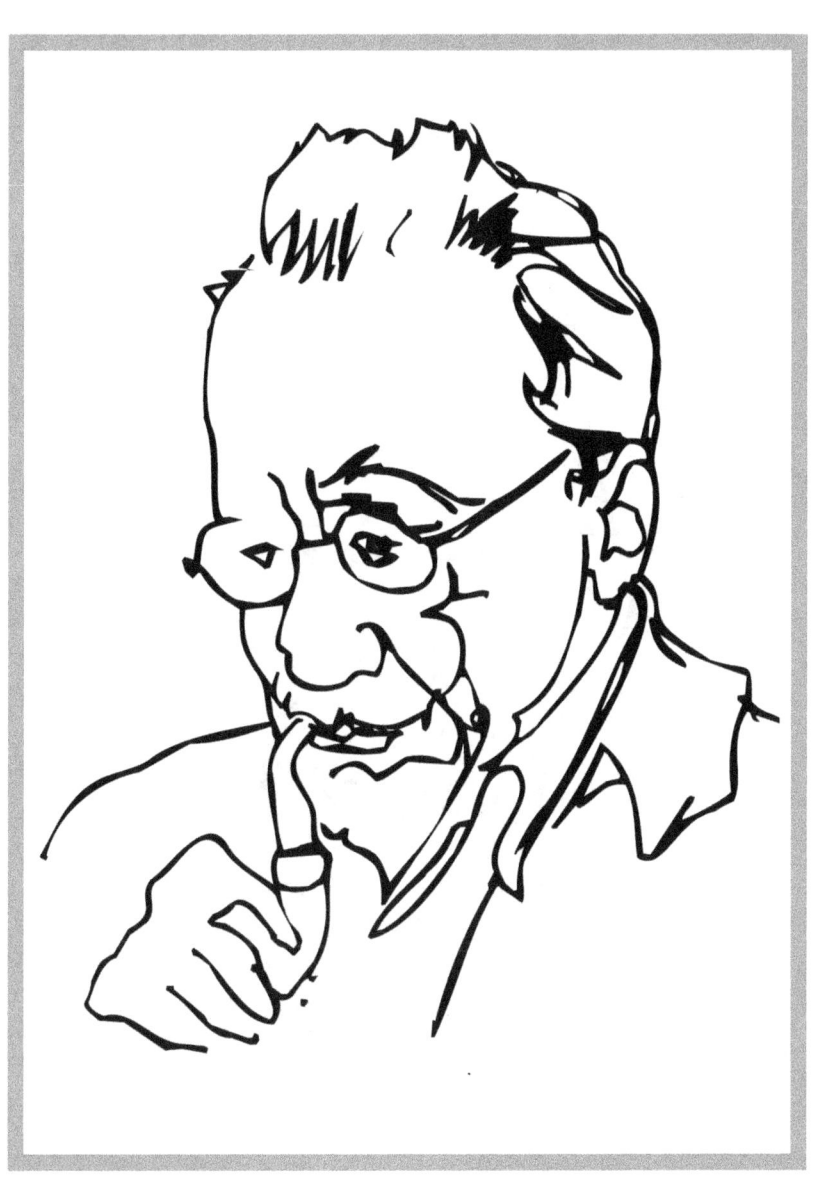

Erwin Schrödinger (1887-1961)

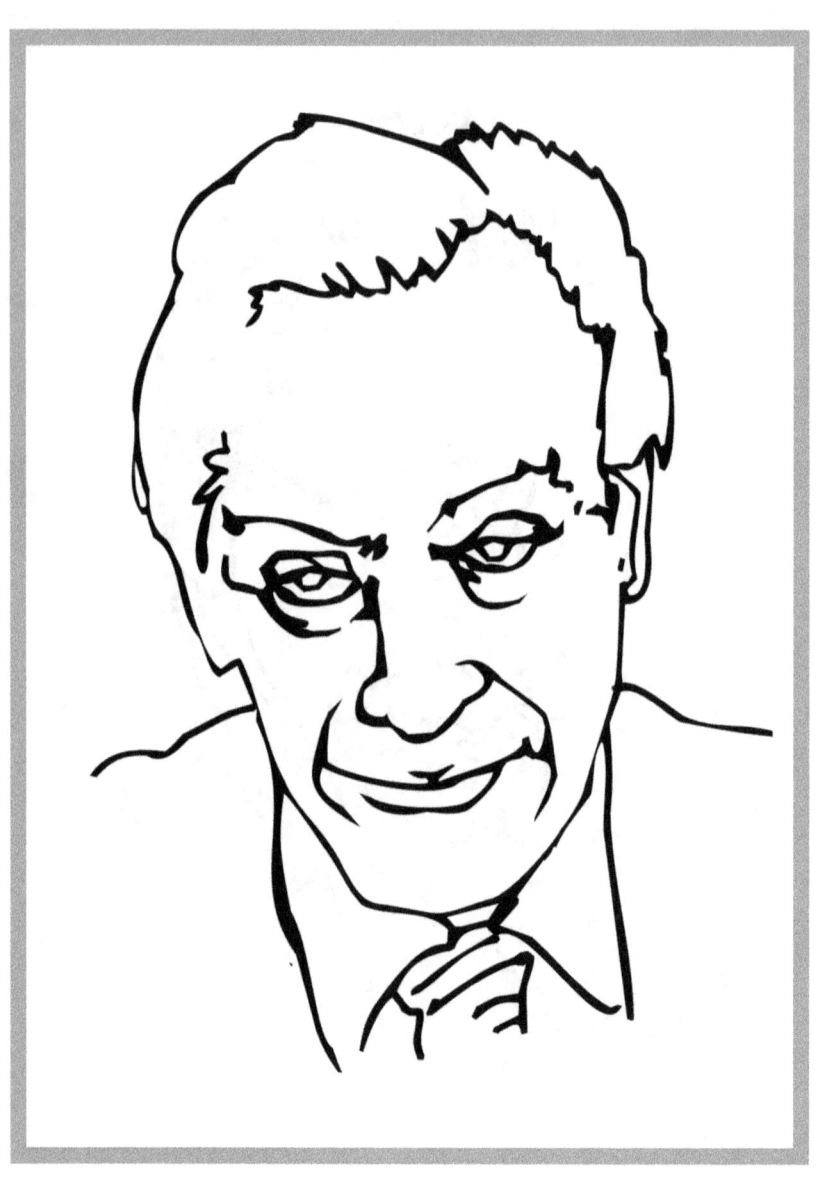

Julian Schwinger (1918-1994)

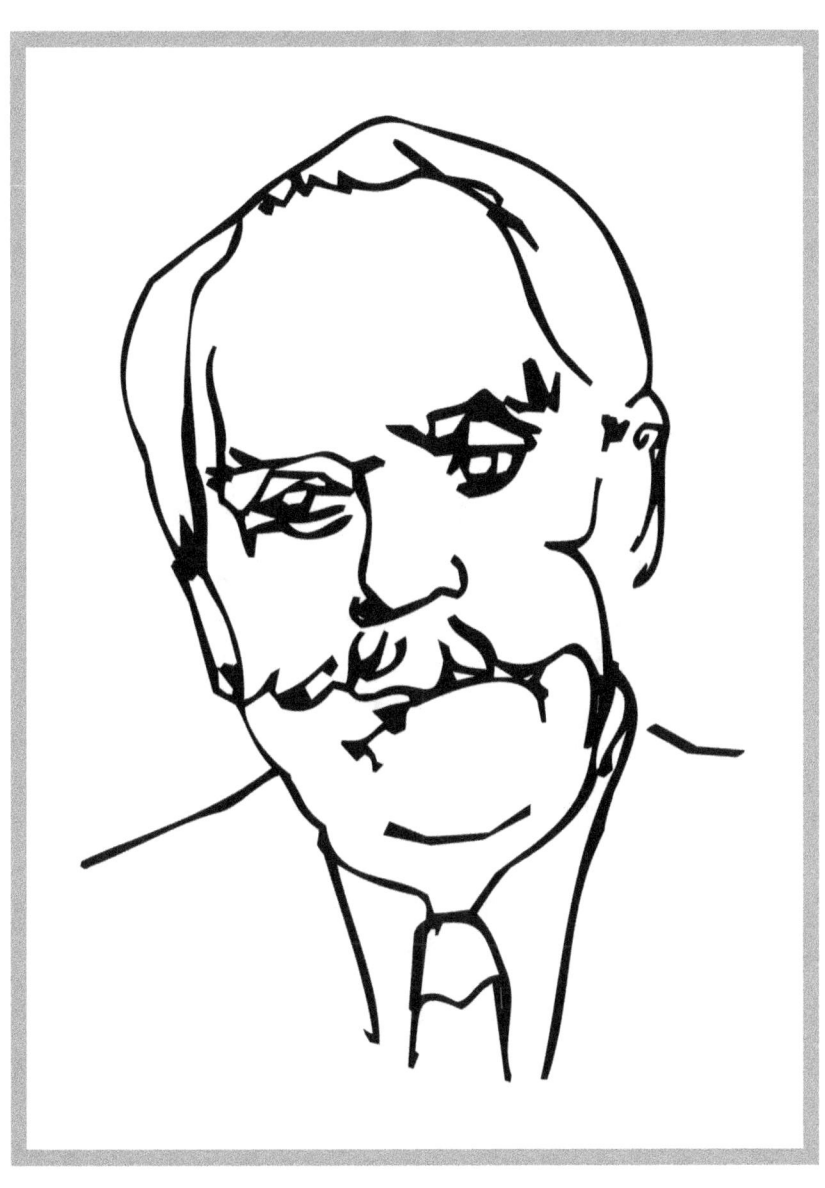

Erwin Rudolf Joseph Alexander Sommerfeld
(1887-1961)

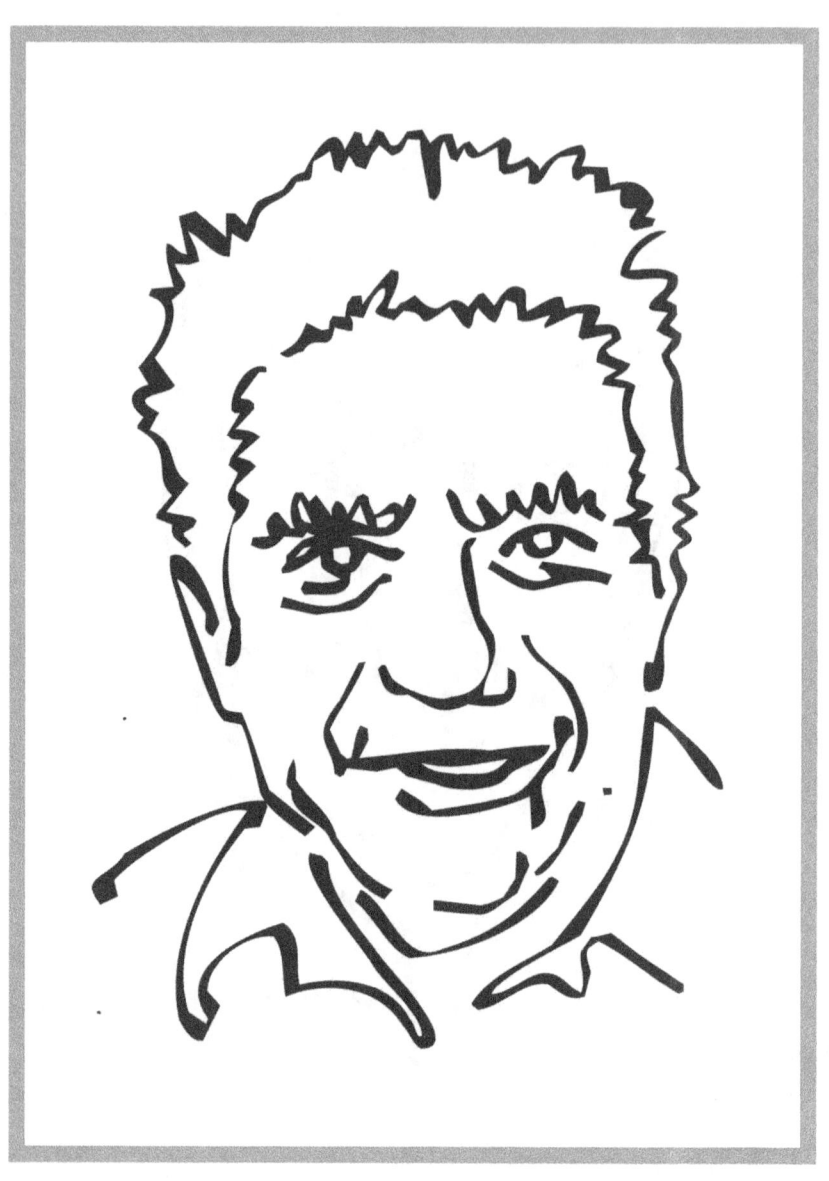

Jack Steinberger (1921...)

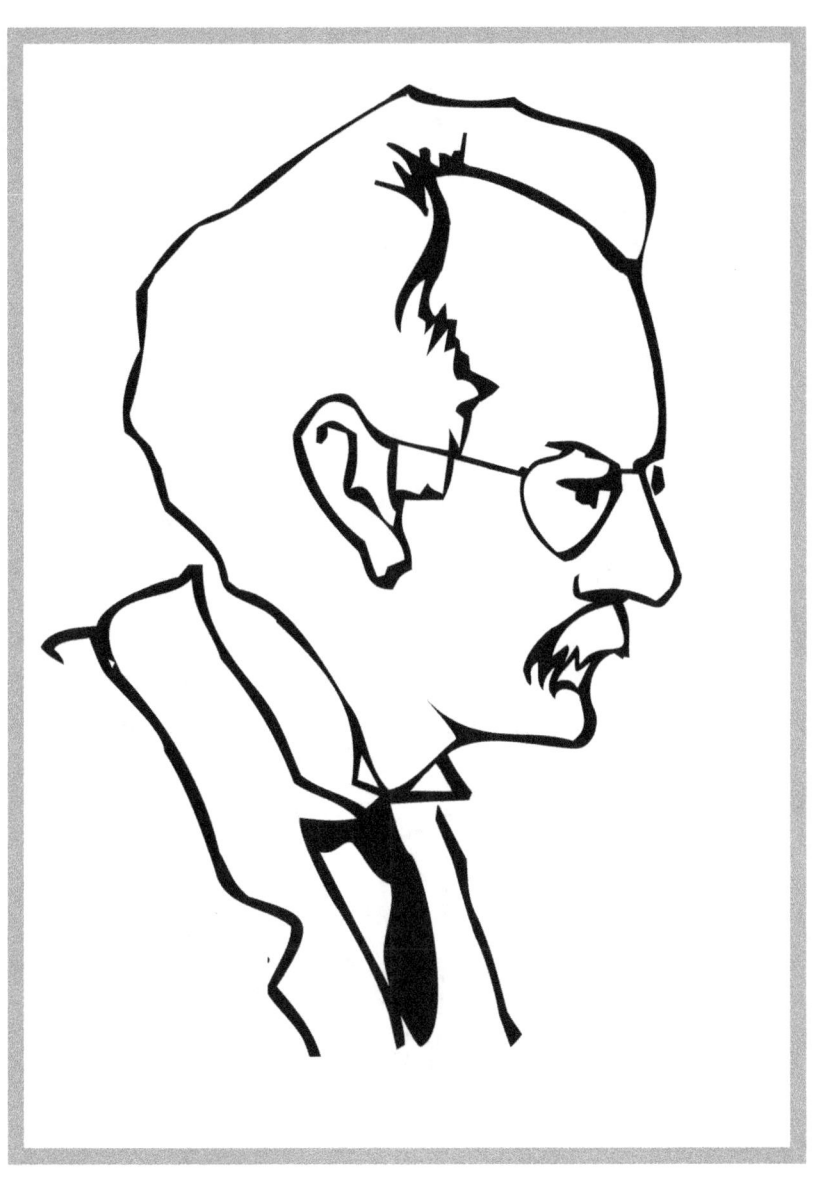

Joseph John Thomson (1856-1940)

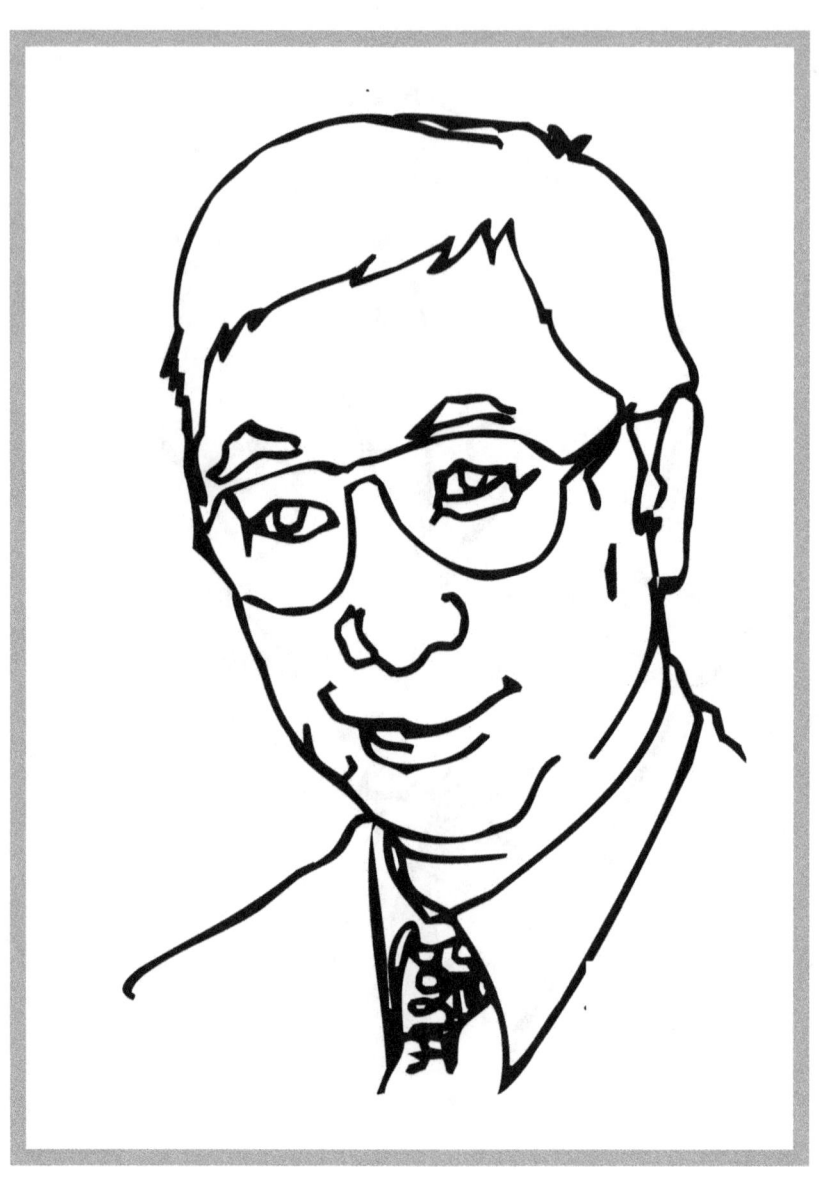

Samuel Chao Chung Ting (1936...)

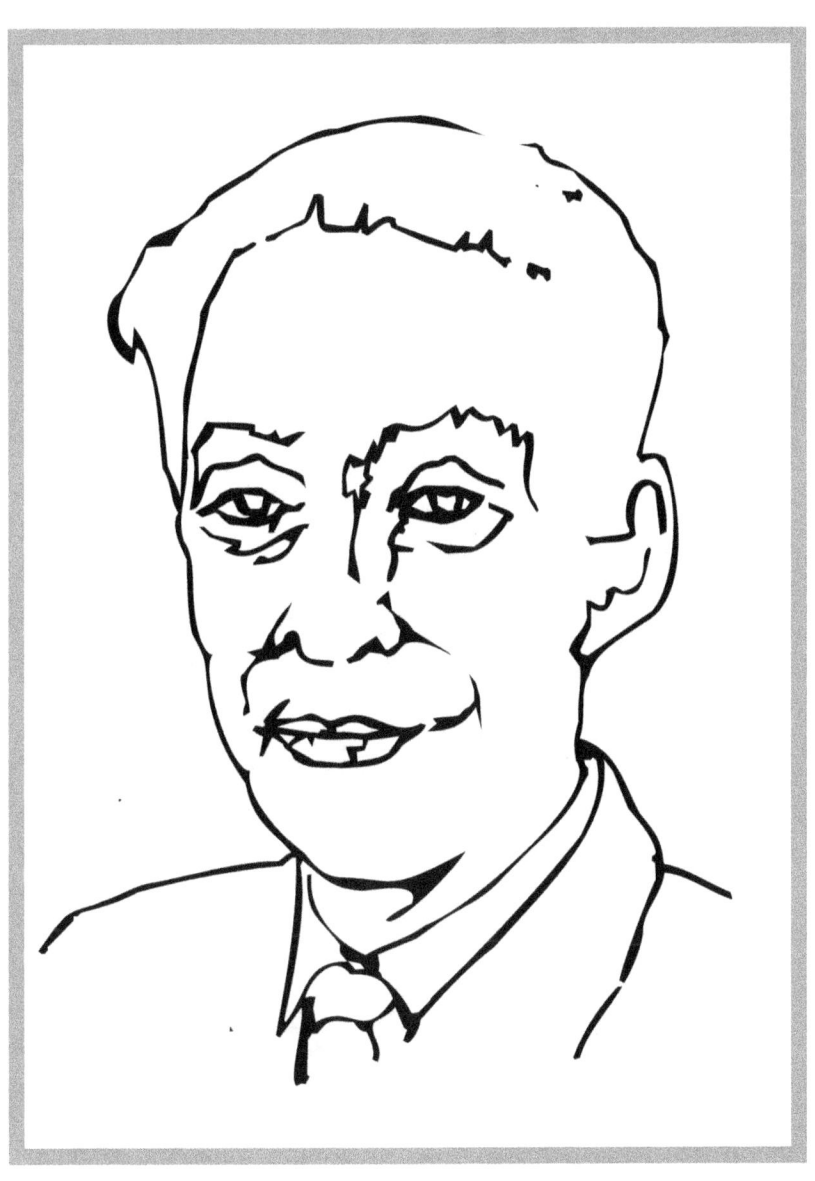

Sin-Itiro Tomonaga (1906-1979)

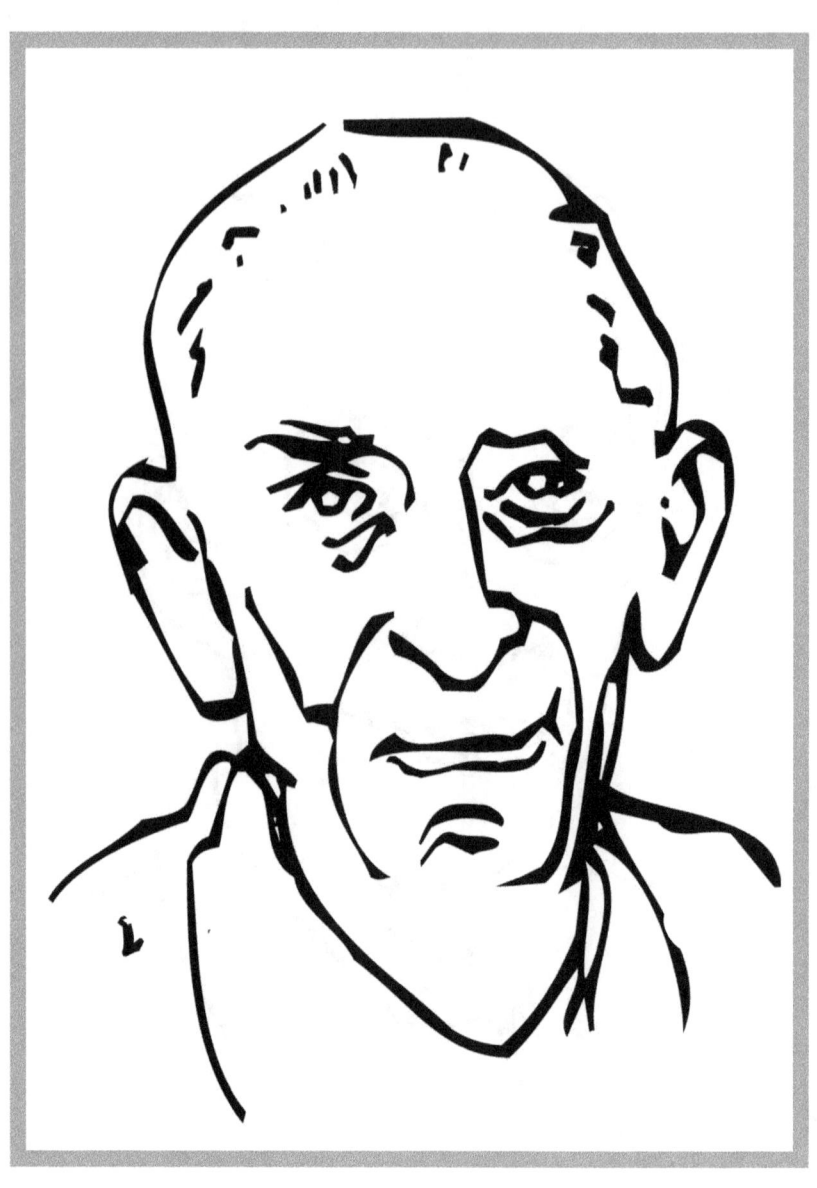

Rolf Wideröe (1902-1996)

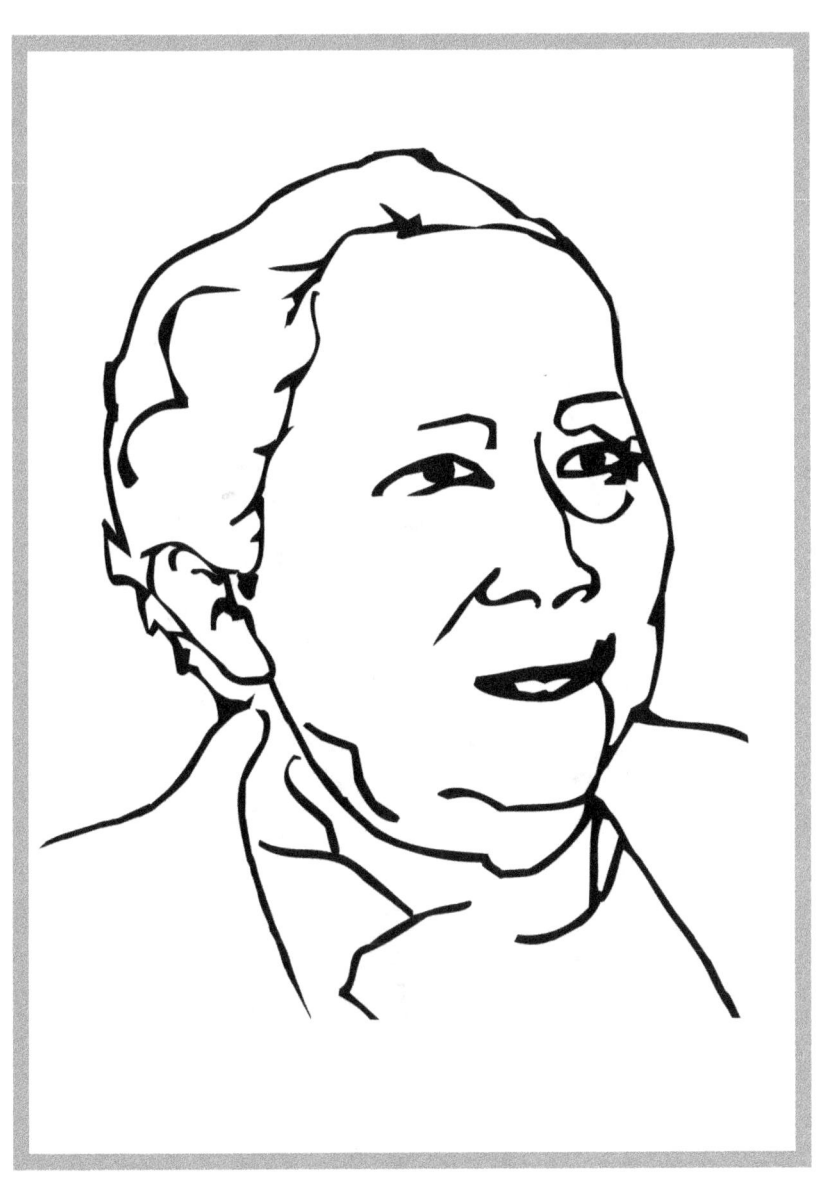

Chien-Shiung Wu (1912-1997)

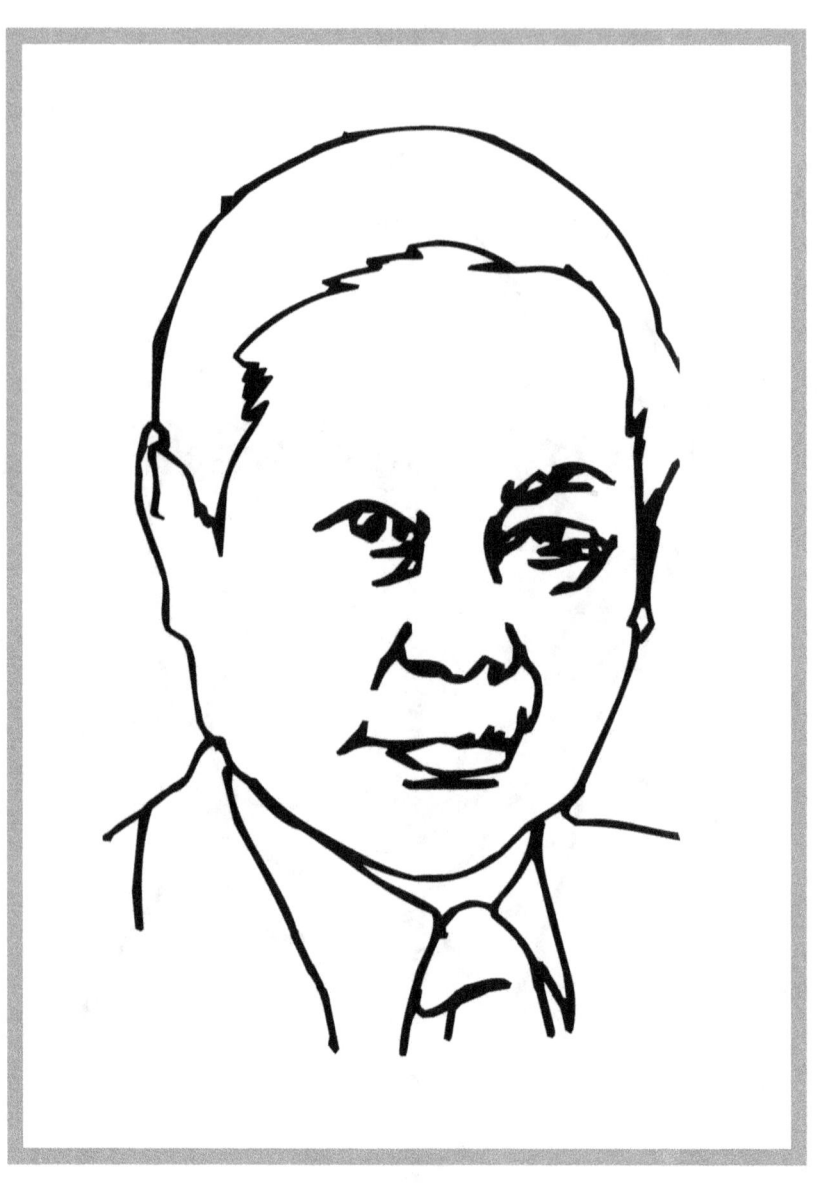

Chen Ning Yang (1922...)

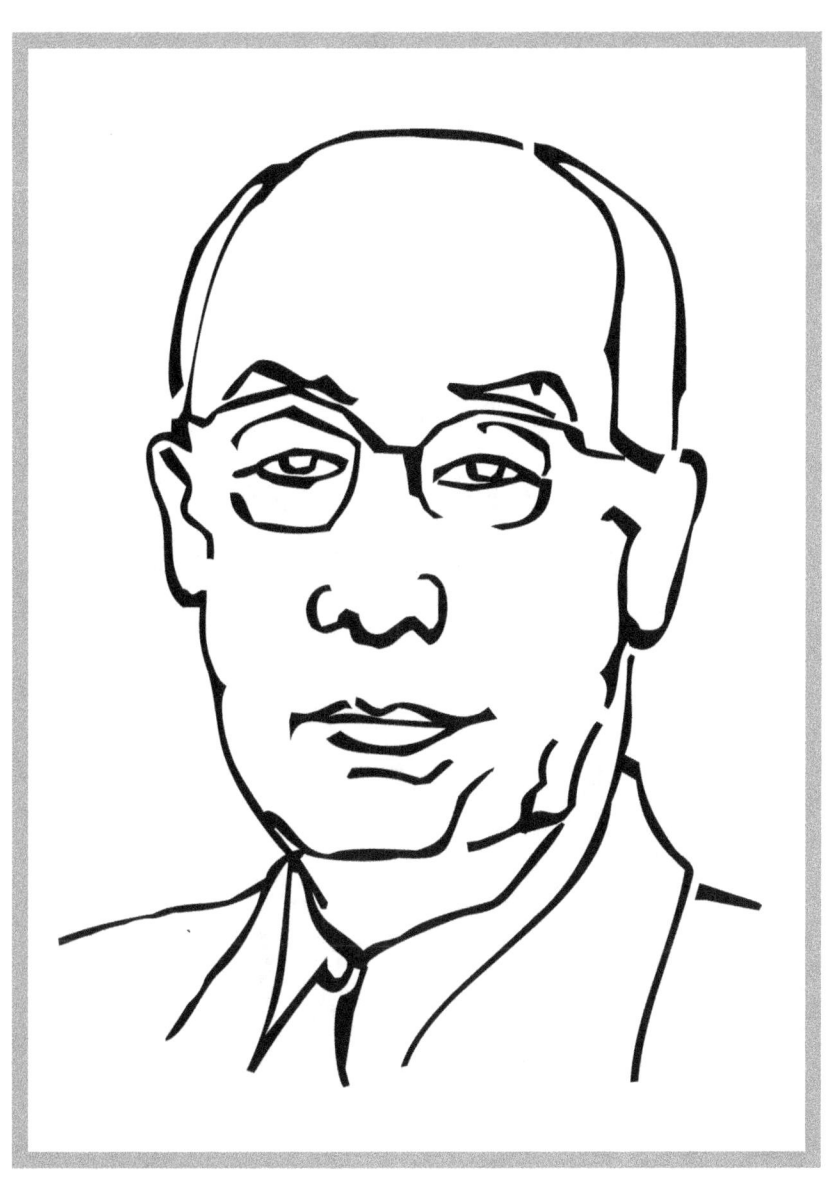

Hideki Yukawa (1907-1981)

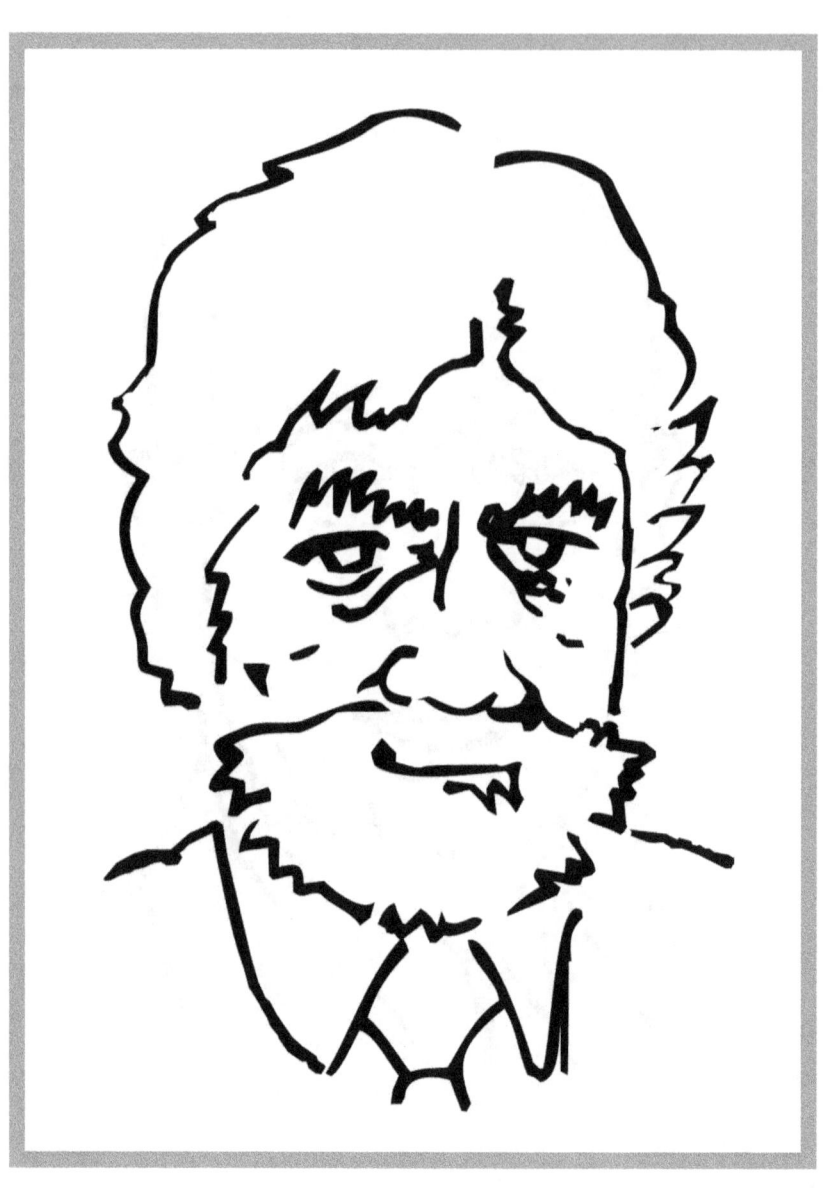

George Zweig (1937...)

Liste der Zeichungen
Lista de dibujos
List of Drawings

iutta zeichnet – *iutta dibujando* – iutta draws 3
Barbara & Pedro 6
Andenexpedition – *Expedición andina* – Expedition to the Andes   10
Ballonflüge – *Vuelos de balones* – Balloon Flights 11
Kernphotoplatten – *Placas nucleares* – Nuclear Emulsions 12
Blasenkammer – *Cámara de burbujas* – Bubble Chamber 13
Cafeteria – *Cafetería* – Cafeteria 14
Wideröe Collider – *Collider* – Collider 15
Zwei Synchrotrons – *Dos sincrotrones* – Two Synchrotrons 16
HERA-Tunnel – *El tunel de HERA* – The HERA Tunnel 16
Beschleuniger – *Aceleradores* – Accelerators 17
Verdrahtung – *Cablage* – Cabling 18
Zeit-Justierung – *Ajustando el „timing"* – Adjusting the Timing 19
Großexperiment – *Experimento* – Experiment 20
Schichtbetrieb – *Físicos „de turno"* – Physicist „on Shift" 21
Schichtende – *Fin de turno* – The End of the Shift 22
Rechenzentrum – *Centro de cálculo* – Computing Centre 23
Labor-Kantine – *Cantina de laboratorio* – Laboratory Canteen 24
Vortrag – *Explicación* – Talk for Visitors 25
Arbeiten zu Hause – *Trabajo en casa* – Working at Home 26
Kein Kommentar – *Sin comentario* – No Comment 27
Standard-Modell – *Modelo standard* – Standard Model 28
Nr. 158 von H1 – *Nr. 158 de H1* – Nr 158 of H1 30
Gruppenvereinigung – *Grupos se juntan* – Groups Unite 31
Köpfe und Hände – *Cabezas y manos* – Heads and Hands. 32
Globalisierung – *Globalización* – Globalization 33
Kraft zusammen – *Fuerza de la unión* – The Power of Unity 34
Pyramide – *Pirámide* – Pyramid 35
Wegweisende Hand – *La mano que guía* – Guiding Hand 36
Grupensprecher – *Speaker* – The Speaker 37
Gesichter und Hände – *Caras y manos* – Faces and Hands 37
Vereinte Gesichter – *Caras unidas* – United Faces 38
Vereinte Hände – *Manos unidas* – United Hands 39
Zusammenstellung – *Composición* – Compilation 40

Liste der Porträts – *Lista de retratos* – List of Portraits 102

Porträts – *Retratos* – Portraits

Anderson 42	Lorentz 72
Becquerel 43	Maxwell 73
Bohr (1) 44	Meer, van der 74
Bohr (2) 45	Millikan 75
Braun, K.F. 46	Nambu 76
Charpak 47	Ne'eman 77
Cowan 48	Newton (1) 78
Dalton 49	Newton (2) 79
Broglie, de 50	Pauli 80
Demokrit 51	Perl 81
Dirac 52	Planck (1) 82
Einstein 53	Planck (2) 83
Fermi (1) 54	Reines 84
Fermi (2) 55	Richter 85
Feynman (1) 56	Rubbia 86
Feynman (2) 57	Rutherford 87
Fritzsch 58	Salam 88
Galileo 59	Schrödinger 89
Geiger 60	Schwinger 90
Gell-Mann 61	Sommerfeld 91
Glashow 62	Steinberger 92
Hahn 63	Thomson, J.J. 93
Heisenberg 64	Ting 94
Helmhotz 65	Tomonaga 95
Hertz 66	Wideröe 96
Hofstadter 67	Wu 97
Lawrence 68	Yang 98
Lederman 69	Yukawa 99
Lee, T.-D. 70	Zweig 100
Lenard 71	

iutta, kurzer Lebenslauf

Die österreichische Künstlerin Jutta Waloschek, die auch unter dem Namen „iutta maría de las manos" bekannt ist, wurde 1931 in Dresden geboren, ist in Argentinien aufgewachsen und hat ihr Studium für Kunsterziehung und Malerei in Buenos Aires und in Wien absolviert. In beiden Städten hat sie heute ein Atelier. Über 120 Einzel- und Gemeinschaftsausstellungen, mehrere Auszeichnungen und Stipendien zeugen von ihrer Produktivität und ihrem künstlerischen Engagement. Neben der Herstellung von Aquarellen, Ölbildern, Zeichnungen und Buch-Illustrationen betätigt sich Jutta besonders auf dem Gebiet der Textilgestaltung, sowohl mit großen Stoffkollagen (Wandbehänge), wie auch mit farbenfrohen Seidenmalereien. Daneben hat Jutta aber nie ihre pädagogischen Fähigkeiten vernachlässigt und sich besonders der künstlerischen Ausbildung von Kindern gewidmet.

iutta, datos biográficos

La artista austríaca Jutta Waloschek, también conocida como „iutta maría de las manos", nació en Dresde (Alemania) en 1931 y pasó su juventud en la Argentina. Completó su educación como enseñante de arte y pintura en Buenos Aires y en Viena. En ambas ciudades mantiene un atelier. Más de 120 exposiciones (entre individuales y colectivas), varios premios y diversas becas demuestran su productividad y su intenso entusiasmo por el arte. Además de realizar innumerables acuarelas, óleos, dibujos e ilustraciones de libros, Jutta es particularmente activa en el campo del arte textil, sea en la manufactura de grandes tapices murales (en técnica de aplicación), como en pintura sobre seda. Jutta siempre continuó con sus actividades didácticas, especialmente en el campo de la educación artística infantil.

iutta, Short Biography

The Austrian artist Jutta Waloschek, also known as 'iutta maría de las manos', was born in Dresden in 1931 and grew up in Argentina. She studied art and trained as an art teacher in Buenos Aires and Vienna, two cities where she and her work continue to be based today. A prolific and enthusiastic artist, she has shown her work in more than 120 individual and collective exhibitions and has been awarded several prizes and scholarships. In addition to her watercolours, oil paintings, drawings and book illustrations, Jutta has a particular interest in textile design (appliqué), and has created numerous large-scale wall hangings and vibrant silk paintings. Jutta has also maintained her keen interest in art education, in particular for children.

Die Farbenpracht der Werke und das künstlerische Talent seiner Schwester Jutta (iutta) haben den Autor dazu verleitet 116 Reproduktionen ihrer Schöpfungen als Büchlein zu veröffentlichen. Es entstand ein Augenschmaus, ideal zum Genießen, zum Nachdenken und vielleicht auch zum Verschenken.
Texte auf Deutsch, Spanisch und Englisch.
Textos en alemán, castellano e inglés.
Texts in German, Spanish and English.

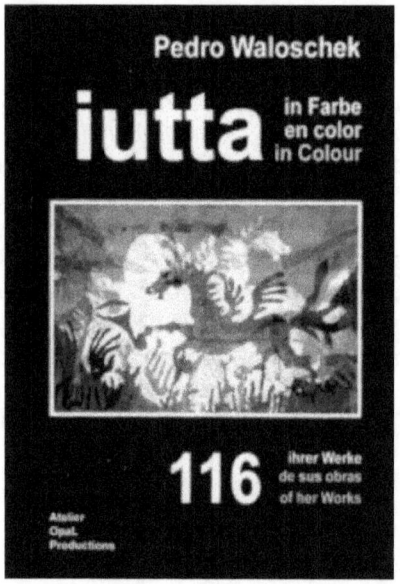

BoD GmbH (2004), 108 Seiten in Farbe, A5.
Im Buchhandel und in
Internet-Buchshops zu bestellen

Paperback, ISBN 3-8334-1497-9 22,- Euro

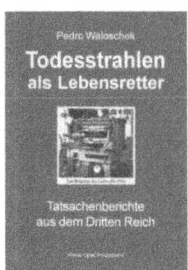

Pedro Waloschek
Todesstrahlen als Lebensretter
Tatsachenberichte aus dem Dritten Reich

Die Ergebnisse jahrelanger Recherchen des Autors werden hier akkurat, aber leicht verständlich und unterhaltsam dargestellt. Es handelt sich um einen wichtigen Beitrag zur Geschichte der Teilchenbeschleuniger in Deutschland. Alle Quellen werden angegeben, einschließlich noch nie veröffentlichte Daten über streng geheime Entwicklungen für Hitlers „Wunderwaffen" und deren Verrat an die Alliierten.

Inhaltsverzeichnis:
Vorwort 7
1 Das Jahr 1943 11
2 Science-Fiction und Realität 19
3 Richard Gans und
   Heinz Schmellenmeiers „Rheotron" 33
4 Ernst Schiebolds „Röntgenkanonen" 65
5 Rolf Widerões „Strahlentransformatoren" 105
6 Das Ende der „Röntgenkanonen" 131
7 Das letzte „Betatron" der Luftwaffe 161
Anhang: Konrad Gunds „Elektronenschleuder" 185
Ein chronologischer Überblick 197
Quellen- und Literaturverzeichnis 211
Personen- und Sachregister 227

BoD GmbH (2004), 240 S., 20 Abb., Format A5,
Hardcover, ISBN 3-8334-0979-7 (34,- Euro),
Paperback, ISBN 3-8334-1616-5 (15,90 Euro).

Der Norweger **Rolf Widerøe** (1902-1996), ein genialer und talentierter Forscher und Entwickler, hätte nach Meinung vieler Fachleute einen Nobelpreis verdient. Grundlegende Beiträge zum Bau von Teilchenbeschleunigern und zu deren Anwendung in Medizin und Technik sind ihm zu verdanken. Ab 1946 hat er für BBC Basel (CH) „Betatrons" gebaut. Zwanzig Jahre war er Professor an der berühmten ETH Zürich. Gelegentlich wurde ihm vorgeworfen, im Zweiten Weltkrieg für die deutsche Luftwaffe gearbeitet zu haben, wofür er aber in seiner Autobiographie recht plausible Gründe anführen konnte.

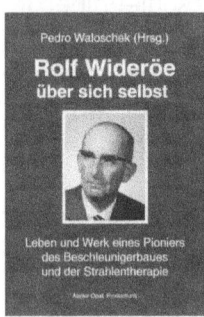

Pedro Waloschek (Hrsg.)

Rolf Widerøe über sich selbst

Leben und Werk eines Pioniers des Beschleunigerbaues und der Strahlentherapie

Widerøes Originaltexte, ein historisches Dokument!
Sonderausgabe als Hardvover
mit Lesebändchen und Schutzumschlag
BoD GmbH (2004), 203 S. 48 Abb. Format A5, ISBN 3-8334-0804-9 (33,- Euro).

Eine Liste der Bücher von Pedro Waloschek
und viel Information über
die Künstlerin **iutta waloschek** (Wien-Buenos Aires)
und den Architekten **Hans Waloschek** (1899-1985)
findet man im Internet unter:
www.waloschek.de

Rund 5500 Stichwörter informieren wissenschaftlich exakt und zugleich allgemeinverständlich über die wichtigsten Themenbereiche der klassischen und neueren Physik. Alle Stichwörter sind mit englischer Übersetzung angegeben. Mit einem englisch-deutschen Verweisregister und 128 Abbildungen.

dtv
Wörterbuch Physik
Von Pedro Waloschek

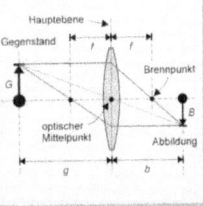

Deutscher Taschenbuch Verlag (dtv) 1998, 586 S.
Im Buchhandel und in Internet-Buchshops
ISBN 3-423-32512-7   14,50 Euro

www.ingramcontent.com/pod-product-compliance
Lightning Source LLC
Chambersburg PA
CBHW070305230526
45470CB00002B/725